Table of Contents

LIFE

AFTER

SCHIZOPHRENIA

ANDERS M. SVENNING

Scarlet Leaf

2019

LIFE AFTER SCHIZOPHRENIA

© 2019 by Scarlet Leaf

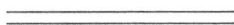

———————————

PUBLISHED BY SCARLET LEAF

Toronto, Canada

Preface

MICROCOSM WITHIN MICROCOSM, the common conception of reality is a blended and converging compilation of global life as common man knows it. But, reality is only half of the whole. The term schizophrenia in its Greek roots, which are schizein, meaning to split, and phren, meaning mind, connote a mind divided or torn apart, or, as Paul Eugen Bleuler, the psychiatrist who coined the term schizophrenia, put it, a "splitting of the psychic functions." No different is the infinite and timeless continuum in which man lives and through which man operates.

Newton's cradle knocks one ball, casts momentum through the subsequent immobile balls, and sends the ball on the opposite end of the cradle into motion. It is physical, the intricate parts of this organic machine, and yet it is emotional, mental, and spiritual. One can state the causal and effectual spheres through which all Animalia, plant life, microscopic phenomena, the atmosphere of earth, cosmology, wars and political and social movement are all related to Albert Einstein's theory of Brownian motion. One's action affects the other and sometimes the effects are separated by mindful units of measurement and sometimes the effects are not what they seem at face value. This is the essential human element—the deception and the semblance and the candid aspects of existence—which courses through man and which is changing with radicalness.

This notion is well acknowledged by many individuals around the world but many are wistful and lackadaisical and drift rather wanton through the scape of contentedness. Some individuals, however, do not float through that scape absent of opinion, passion, and motivation.

I tend to be one of the individuals of the latter sort, that is I have seen, been subject to, and have been transformed as a result of the radical changes which have occurred around the globe in just the past fifteen or twenty years. This book is aimed to appeal to the reader who like me has noticed this change and are dissatisfied by it; but more so this book is aimed at the maturing, broadening populace affected, a part of, or plain interested in the hysterical phenomenon growing with rapidity known as schizophrenia.

I realize the transformation of a populace's opinion as a whole is near impossible and to attempt to change the belief systems of an individual or group of people would be vain and hypocritical as per the notions of freewill and individualism contained within this book. Instead, the aim of writing this book was to affect not a group of people but the individual who is a part of the greater, or macrocosmic group, putting into context via the successive content herein one's own infinitesimal existence beside the global, the universal, and the transcendental realms through which all operate. The smallness, size, or infinitesimal existence of the individual is far too the case and can be rather scary. But, this actualization being discussed at present is necessary for the individual's homeostatic nature and dominance which are naturalistic mechanisms in not only the human being but all living beings and in some cases even in non-living beings. The scape between macrocosms and microcosms, consciousness and subconsciousness, the wizened perception and the latent perception, and just as well any other different, or dissimilar notions is tenuous at best and can even be hazardous. There are bridges, spaces, channels and devices, notions, actions, words and languages which can expedite and incite this shift of consciousness and which are described in length in this book. Schizophrenia, however, is the context in which such phenomenon, experiences, or sensations will be discussed; the baseless claim that an individual is experiencing hallucinations and delusions is a hasty and careless conclusion when in fact the sensations and perceptions experienced are of a spiritual and religious nature which to the commoner, or layman are quite unexplainable. This mystery has not been discussed for some time, not since the psychological renaissance of the early- and mid-twentieth century. This book aims to rekindle the introspective and creative minds of the individual, from one identifying as a mental health professional, a commoner, or layman interested in mental disease, spirituality, and religion, and even those who have been, as is much too often the case, misdiagnosed with schizophrenia.

Anders M. Svenning

Tampa, Florida

30 May 2017

Introduction

The book you are now reading breaks down the theory, or thought form schizophrenia into many different levels starting with the opening essay which is titled, "Schizophrenia: Real or Imagined." The science known as ontology which delineates the bases of existence is a device used to further scrutinize schizophrenia from the oblique angle of those diagnosed, or as put in this book misdiagnosed as per misconstrued symptoms which are spiritual and religious in origin.

Individuals many times are taken against their will to mental health offices and even institutionalized for deviant thoughts which are in turn verbalized and which are in all of actuality the subconscious surfacing and in effect initiating pansophism in the individual which is as C.G. Jung has put it the ultimate objective of man as an individual and as a whole. The book has throughout its pages a subtle theme of metaphysical faith, spirituality, and even religiosity in context with the scientific decomposition of schizophrenia from ontological systems of thought and the characteristics of belief systems and elements of belief systems—all of which tend to work converse to the intentions, conscious and subconscious, of the so called psychotic individual as per the power imbalance present in the mental health sphere and the transposition of faith to a more synthetic and solvated knowledge domain.

Exchanges between spiritual and religious advanced individuals and mental health professionals, those misdiagnosed with schizophrenia in society and in functional groups of people following the misfortunate donning of the illness, Jungian psychology regarding the soul and embodied cognition are all notions pursued in the following pages and take the reader on a fantastic trial through the subconscious intentions of misdiagnosed schizophrenic individuals, or spiritual and religious advanced individuals in the context of timeless mythology and contemporary anecdotes. The hindering of pansophism and even the hindering of corporeal atonement with one's subconscious is perpetuated through the intellectual and monetary vacuum that is the pharmaceutical industry, misplaced faith systems in mental health professionals, and the willingness, or gullibility of many misdiagnosed individuals and those individuals' families who have been affected by schizophrenia; this hindered pansophism is aimed to be counter-balanced with the theory depicted within these pages and which lies down the collinear processes of the how and the why regarding the schizophrenic thought form, its prevalence, and its recent transformation into hysteria by incorporating the individualistic, societal, spiritual, and even religious causations of supposed schizophrenic ideas, or symptoms.

Supplements for mental unstable individuals today are not natural chemicals. They are synthetic pills and solutions made in laboratories. Most means of treatment and even cognitive therapeutic ideology in the twenty-first century are not sufficient. Medication administered to misdiagnosed schizophrenic patients is not a remedy.

It is not sunlight which descends UVB-rays and upon contact with the skin transforms into vitamin D which is needed for calcium absorption and which optimizes magnesium in the bloodstream. It is not a staple in the Mediterranean diet which has a high concentration of vitamin A, selenium, zinc, iodine, and iron, amongst other nutrients. It is not olive oil which is comprised of fatty acids good for the nervous system, the circulatory system, and just as well any and all internal body systems. It is not a catalyst to a genuine mind-body effect given by herbal supplements such as sarsaparilla, Hawaiian baby woodrose, and valerian root.

These chemicals are created in laboratories within American metropolises and metropolises around the world.

Let me tell you about disfigurement. Personality traits following a misdiagnosis of schizophrenia and subsequent treatment fall away. Identities slide into changed compositions. The shift from former to latter self as a result of a misdiagnosis of schizophrenia are not only traumatic on an introspective level but also in an outward and more colloquial level.

A shift not toward uniformity but a shift toward a high and true countenance which is a universal goal and aspiration in man and which is the be all and end all of this book is an action that can take place not only in an individual but in a global society. It is left up to the perceptive populace to take the initiative.

LIFE AFTER SCHIZOPHRENIA

Social trends and monetary trends in the world are much like habitual trends in a person. Sir Isaac Newton's experimentations in the mid-seventeenth century and his subsequent results are quite relevant and have been published in his 1686 publication *Principia Mathematica Philosophiæ Naturalis* which depicts Newton's three laws of motion. The first of which reads as follows: An object at rest stays at rest and an object in motion stays in motion with the same speed and in the same direction unless acted upon by an unbalanced force. This is also known as the law of inertia and is true of material objects but also true of social movements and ideologies and internal spirituality and religious realizations. Obstacles will be met, contended with, and are quite omnipresent. But, the words herein are a debunk of misdirected belief systems regarding schizophrenia and a proclamation not only of potential in the schizophrenic populace but also in the global populace for humanistic pansophism.

Schizophrenia: Real or Imagined

———

THERE SEEMS TO BE A divide between two macrocosmic forces which differentiate and separate two very different belief systems. One: the belief systems of the misdiagnosed schizophrenic patients. And two: the belief systems of the mental health professionals and their backers. This schismatic crevasse one could describe as terminal and fatalistic to the human in its very foundations and just as well many more manifestations of humanity—art, philosophy, and basic humanitarian exchanges included. This divide, or crevasse is the device which is used albeit unbeknownst by its propagators to end in man the state of beauty, wonderment, and individuality, all of which are the very derivatives of childhood, innocence, and purity.

Schizophrenia is said to be a schism in the minds of the patients of mental health professionals but it is also a schism in the very society, economy, and even religious elements which too propagate a so-called and ideal humanitarianism. The delineation between the healthy and the unhealthy has become vague, dull, and grayed out by hasty diagnoses and prognoses and a blind following of a theory of psychology and state of mind otherwise known as schizophrenia.

First, what comes to mind when thinking in terms perhaps unaccepted by common people and those established in the mental health professional field is the basis on which this rather heinous notion has become founded, that is a categorical ordaining of a people and classification of a state of mind into one which has become with unfortunateness ugly and dejected. While some with the diagnosis of schizophrenia wield their diagnosis like flora in the face of a hateful, subjective world others are battling with an internal schism not of the mind but of the heart—are they really as the mental professional says schizophrenic? Is this term of classification of a people on a generalized scale just? Is it effective and worthy? Is it based at all on actual evidence or is the diagnosis of schizophrenia a mere speculation which has come to fruition and been embraced by not only mental health professionals but by laypeople around the world? The introspective and intelligent individual with such a life terminating or life delaying diagnosis might think this last question on a level deep within one's faculties for introspection and come to realize that the answer to the question is no. Schizophrenia is not me. It never was. Schizophrenia is a short coming of all I have ever worked for and all I have ever become. It is not that with which I wished to cohabitate nor was it at all what I wished for those around me—family, friends, and coworkers who might attempt to redirect my beliefs into a sphere which cannot be called my own but a sphere that is incompatible with the development of self and created on a level and by a people who are microscopic in understanding and who are rather ingratiating, family and friends and coworkers who might change their views on me if I were to stand up for myself, my individuality all the while using a comprehensive thought process and not swallowing every notion, diagnosis, or pill without a sense of the timeless phenomena *cogito ergo sum*, or I think, therefore I am.

LIFE AFTER SCHIZOPHRENIA

Those critical and thinking about the universal concept of schizophrenia may find themselves musing if schizophrenia is an actual thing, item, or identity or if it was imagined, or invented for the purpose of classifying a people with deviant ideas and who voiced their thoughts. As stated, there is a schism between those who believe in schizophrenia and those who do not believe in schizophrenia. But, perhaps looking into a notion as abstract as schizophrenia from a literal and direct perspective is ineffective and rather vain. Instead, employing theories and concepts from high-thinkers of the past would be better in regards to a lens through which to look at and dissect schizophrenia, the first and most relevant lens being the very foundation of reality and the implementation of words to signify, or symbolize an idea or object.

It is said that concepts, that is ideas extracted from the imaginative sphere, or locale are units of measurement in regards to knowledge domains. The study of trees can be broken down into many different kinds from deciduous trees to palm trees. Fauna, that is the Animalia which keep us company and which thrive in their own habitat and in their own regard from Lepidoptera to Ornethuræ to Canis lupus familiars are all sub-divisions of the greater macrocosm, or knowledge domain known as zoology. Architecture, too, can be sub-divided into devices such as the dome, the arch, and the column and can be studied in a practical and applicable sense but also in a historical context. These concepts ranging from lichen to fauna to manmade architecture are all unitary measurements in knowledge domains. They are actual objects and can be studied on a material, or corporeal level and even on a temporal level when viewing such concepts through a historical lens. Insofar as schizophrenia—which is rather blatant, candid, and separate of actuality and its foundations as the reader will be shown below—the ethereal concept, or idea of the desultory, unattractive diagnosis schizophrenia is susceptible to dismemberment from a logical standpoint, a socio-economic normative standpoint, and even a religious standpoint. But, before getting into the key points, or elements of the belief system and before the definitions of reality and actuality are separated and defined one must set forth a simplistic and unequivocal foundation for dismembering the debilitating conception of schizophrenia, a foundation which will demolish the notion much as the foundation of schizophrenia has been built and has damaged the world in which we live on an intellectual, societal, and spiritual and religious level.

It was written in a straightforward and fundamental article titled "Ontology: Several Theories on the Representation of Knowledge Domains" by de Almeida Campos and Gomes that:

> Wüster's theory of concepts was destined for failure, and it produces major confusion with heavy consequences in medical informatics projects. Smith argues that concepts are not clearly defined and that definition is seldom viewed as the meaning resulting from a cognitive process, for instance, as a form of knowledge in the mind of a specialist or as a term in a system. Problems then arise because

simultaneous attempts are made to use the same term for navigating relationships between different entities of the real world.

It tends to be the case that de Almeida Campos and Gomes when writing their article were correct in regards to Wüster's theory of concepts for the very reason written above. Abstract, or ethereal thought forms are not able to be actualized, or confirmed based on physical characters and common denominators which can and should be the identifying factors for anything "real." Reality and actuality are in fact two very different qualities, or aspects of existence. Reality and actuality are the two poles of existence which create a dichotomy that corrugates knowledge domains. Reality is the word one uses to explain the pole of existence concerned with the naming of concepts and items. Take the deciduous tree and the palm tree, the Lepidoptera and Ornethuræ and Canis lupus familiaris, the dome and the arch and the column for instance. These are all very "real" concepts and their names are the "real" representation of their "actual" existences. In all actuality, however, the deciduous tree and palm tree are pigmented and filled with chlorophyll in their leaves. There is fiber in their bark and in the soil in which they are rooted. The Lepidoptera have powder on their wings which when touched leave granular stains on the fingers. Ornethuræ are light weight and capable of flight as per their hollow bone structure and plumage. Canis lupus familiaris are quadrupeds and have tails which wag back and forth when in ambivalent moods. These are all representations of an idea's, or concept's actualities. That which the words represent are physical, or material and are present in the corporeal world. Going so far as to state that schizophrenia as a broad concept was "destined for failure" (De Almeida Campos and Gomes) from the very beginning is in absolute harmony with the delineation between reality and actuality. Schizophrenia is also destined for failure as per de Almeida Campos's and Gomes's observation that there would be "heavy consequences in medical informatics projects" (De Almeida Campos and Gomes). That schizophrenia which first surfaced in the minds of psychologists in the nineteenth century has been transmogrified into a term composed of the root word schizo- and the modifier -phrenia, has been birthed insofar as reality, that is a concept, and has been let loose upon the world as a typographical notion, a notion which has developed far more rapid and absolute than its progenitors foresaw, deems it quite real; one must give justice, or regards to the omnipresence of schizophrenia as a concept. But, he or she who acknowledges its omnipresence, or reality can also go so far as to state it is not an actual entity, that is the notion is made of preconceptions and the rejection of deviant ideas by mental health professionals. Its components are whimsical and weightless. For that reason, the development of thoughts and conscious pursuit of schizophrenia as a notion and its dissemination is a battle ready and worthy pursuit.

All this though is mere philosophizing and speculation. What really is the theatre at which schizophrenia operates and is perpetuated is the theatre of belief. Belief is a strong, powerful feeling one gets and feels in their body and one which takes hold deep and rooted in the mind much like our deciduous tree. When a belief takes hold and its roots stretch so deep and its branches span so wide that its renders all beneath it in a shadow it is hard, or even impossible to mount and triumph over that belief. One can attempt to climb the limbs and one can pick fruit from the tree and eat the fruit but triumphing over a belief so embedded in the soils of society can be a near vain pursuit. In order to escape its shadow one must move from beneath the shelter and travel to a more appropriate and even more lavish locale.

In the quote below, when I first read it, the term that struck me as most powerful was the term "belief" when used in conjunction with reality and actuality and mental entities and knowledge domains. Klein and Smith state in their article:

> In Wüster's theory, a concept is understood as a mental concept, idea, or thought (Aristotle's noesis) that respects a mind state of specific individuals, a state that may be evoked by the use of a correspondent general term. For Smith, this approach is based on a psychological position in which concepts are mental entities, analogously related to ideas and beliefs. This point of view cannot be properly accepted when proposing a standardized terminological system for a domain, since a high degree of arbitrariness and diversity occurs when concepts are constructed in individual minds. Plus, researchers that adopt this position must explain why concepts and their characteristics are either creatures of mind or properties of objects in the world. Thus, it is not clear for individuals creating terminologies whether their elements are

representations of ideas in the mind of individuals, meanings of words, knowledge of specialists as a consensus, or types of entities in the world.

While the fundamental argument set forth thus far in this essay are still present in the above quote the new term, "belief," makes itself known and evident. This is a preponderant and fantastic surfacing of a word that is far removed from science. Belief is untestable. Belief is not empirical. Belief is not a material, or corporeal item. It cannot be set on a weight and in conjunction with another item or another belief be donned to excite or have more gravity or less gravity than the other item of belief. It cannot be measured by a yardstick or an odometer. It cannot be dipped with litmus paper and be called acidic or basic in regards to the color its evokes. It cannot be brought into contact with a thermometer and called hot or cold based on how high the mercury solution within the thermometer rises. Belief cannot be conjured in a laboratory and entice a change in mechanics, biology, or physiognomy. It is a notion, or entity separate from any empirical or numerical significance or semblance. Belief is not made up of chemicals or molecules or positive or negative protons and electrons. It is pure and human and unlike any other concept or idea in the world. Rather than corporeal units with which to measure something so abstract and mysterious as belief we have concepts as representation units in its knowledge domain.

Concepts are bridged by relationships. There are two kinds of relationships as termed by de Almeida Campos and Gomes in their article "Ontology: Several Theories on the Representation of Knowledge Domains": Relationships may be classed into two groups: logical relationships and ontical relationships. The first ones are abstract, and they occur among concepts. The second ones occur among objects contiguous in time or space. It seems to be the case that schizophrenia as an entity is not a candidate for one of the latter relationships, that is ontical relationships, which bridge the gap between reality and actuality. It belongs if at all in the former of the two relationships, which bridges the divide between abstract ideas and their typographical representations. That being said, the concept of schizophrenia is weightless and untrue. One could call the term schizophrenia and its subjective nature, that is the observation and believability of its prerequisites—delusions, hallucinations, and any or all deviant thoughts or behavior spoken or enacted—as inconsistent and absent in terms of adequate relational and contextual characteristics. It has been written in "Ontology: Several Theories on the Representation of Knowledge Domains" by de Almeida Campos and Gomes that there are four inconsistencies when dealing with abstract concepts such as schizophrenia:

Inconsistencies of a different nature found are related here, namely: 1) hierarchical: failure in the structure of concepts; relevant terms missing in the hierarchy; 2) relational: few relationships available to describe relationships among terms and to express domain knowledge; 3) definitional: inadequate text not explicating characteristics and their relationships, preventing/blocking formalism; lack

of patterns for definitions; and, 4) contextual: lack
of documentation of ontologies about their scope,
objective and subject.

I understand there are chemicals in the brain which mental
health professionals seem to believe is the root or source of
all human emotion, decision making, and every other
manifestation under the sun. I understand observations of
misfortunate patients with the diagnosis schizophrenia are
under the push and pull of a great many systems of beliefs set
against and casted upon their own systems of beliefs. It tends to
be the case that mental health professionals take the initiative
in times of introspection oscillating within their patients.
Words spoken to mental health professionals that are not
believable such as verbalized religiosity and mindfulness and
notions regarding global and/or national upheaval and the
unbalanced power scale within the nations or the world at
large are common prerequisites to a diagnosis, or misdiagnosis
of schizophrenia. In fact, he or she who makes the decision
to render an individual ill and who writes down the term
"schizophrenia" on a sheet of A4 paper is in want of a few key
points regarding the lack of

synchronization and dismissiveness of their own belief systems
regarding the diagnosis schizophrenia.

The common claim is that a man or a woman or even a child
who is experiencing a set group of thoughts and are vocalizing
nonsensical ideas and are enacting nonsensical actions are
candidates for the diagnosis schizophrenia. While there are
tests and studies being performed in regards to chemicals in the

brain and schizophrenic patients it seems to be the case that mental health professionals base their decisions in regards to diagnosis on verbalization and in some cases nonsensical acts. So far as mental health professionals are concerned the rousing of both a chemical imbalance in the brain and observable actions and words one can call deviant is ideal when attempting to establish empirical data regarding the diagnosis and supposed symptoms of an individual. The mental health professional when this supposed empirical data is brought together and recorded call this a manifestation of a mental disease. De Almeida Campos and Gomes write:

> Another example of an accurate and precise term related to mental disease is shown in GO[1]: "MANIFESTATION OF A MENTAL DISEASE = def. a BODILY FEATURE of an ORGANISM that is (a) deviation from clinical normality that is the *realization* of a MENTAL DISEASE and is (b) observable." Capital letter characters are characteristics that are also concepts, and as such they are elements of description; relationships are in italics. Characteristics are shown in capital letters; it means that they are also defined.

While this theory is convincing to some people, mental health professionals and laymen alike, it is not compatible with the dichotomy of existence, that is reality and actuality, as a result of the divide separating mental health professionals and the misdiagnosed insofar as belief systems, and it is an untrue theory which widens the fissure between humanity and mechanistic decision making, inconsistent and wasteful.

A study was exacted at the Carmel Workshop on Cognitive Psychophysiology in Australia in the year 2016. The study was a typical study attempting to establish a connection between chemical imbalances in the brain and schizophrenic symptoms—hallucinations, delusions which are classified under many different types and which will be defined in a later essay in this book, and verbalization to hurt one's self or another. While these symptoms are deviant in terms of common accepted thoughts and even actions in society at present they are not innate to a sub-division of thought one can call evil or wrong or immoral, and are not prerequisites for a diagnosis of the vague and misfortunate type called schizophrenia. While there seems to be a fascination with schizophrenic symptoms throughout the world by not only psychologists, psychiatrists, and other scientists but also by those advanced in religious or spiritual practices, the symptoms or supposed effects of schizophrenia or, as medical professionals claim are effects of chemical imbalances in the brain, are rather undermined in terms of application to existence and scorned by professionals and the layman alike. For effects as the Carmel Workshop scientists claim to be "florid psychotic symptoms of hallucinations and delusions" (McCarley) they are attempting with much fervor and anticipation to douse the "florid" phenomena and remove them from the patients' minds which some religious or spiritual individuals might say or think is rather opportune for religious or spiritual development. The phenomena of "floral" symptoms which can be called hallucinations and delusions but which can also be called illumination by Buddhist practitioners and requisites for atonement by Christian monks is further deprecated by a parallel made by an individual named Dr. John Olney regarding the similarities between the spinal cords of test rats and the brains of the diagnosed schizophrenic. Robert W. McCarley writes in his article "Studies from Neuroscience Research Australia Update Current Data on Schizophrenia (Dysregulations of Synaptic Vesicle Trafficking in Schizophrenia): "It is interesting in this regard that the PCP-mediated damage to pyramidal dendritic spines in rats, described by Dr. Olney, mimics the neuropathology observed in the brains of schizophrenia patients." The discovery of this similarity is an uneducated observation and I cannot believe it has been published and used as evidence fortifying the reality of schizophrenia.

Psychology while interesting to me ever since a young age was never a field I wished to pursue nor did I intend to take such progressive and deviant perspectives on the practical aspect of psychology while at that young and virile age but I did take a few psychology classes which I enjoyed and from which I learned much, one of the timeless and proved theories of science learned in my time as a psychology student being the fallacy known as *post hoc ergo propter hoc*, or correlation does not imply causation. The implementation of a drug on a rodent of such a size, weight, gene and blood type cannot with accuracy nor dignity be connected with the brain of an individual with a size, weight, gene and blood type that is human. It is irresponsible and misfortunate that such a correlation has been published but people tend to find fantastical inspiration in making connections that are illogical and have a supposed empirical and material relation and are founded on a corporeal basis.

The Carmel Workshop on Cognitive Psychophysiology was not meant to establish relations between drugged rodents and deviant individuals in mental faculties. The scientists at the Carmel Workshop on Cognitive Psychophysiology were attempting to establish a relation between the mental normative population and the mental deviant population, a relation which was attempted to be bridged with the device known as neurological synaptic vesicles.

The so called effect of dysregulations of synaptic vesicle trafficking is called by mental health professionals schizophrenia, which as stated is incomplete as per its validity and which resides with definitiveness in only two out of five spheres of existence—they are the epistemological sphere of existence and the performative sphere of existence. The scientists at the Carmel Workshop of Cognitive Psychophysiology have attempted to ground synaptic activity in all spheres of existence, the temporal, spatial, corporeal spheres of existence as well as the two sphere of existence in which the empirical study of neuroscience resides undeniable, the epistemological sphere of existence and the performative sphere of existence. Outside the epistemological and performative spheres of existence, the empirical study of neurology and the scientists who are attempting to bridge the gap between chemicals in the brain and the diagnosis schizophrenia and who are convinced in full of its prevalence will need help from a metaphysical source one could call religious to prove without doubt that the connection between neuroscience and dysregulations of synaptic vesicle trafficking in schizophrenia and the diagnosis of schizophrenia are in semblance and true. The disembodiment of schizophrenia and the definitions of the five spheres of existence as told from Paul James, a writer on globalization, sustainability, and social theory, will be differentiated below. But before we dissect schizophrenia from an ontological perspective as told by Paul James, we will dissect a fatal error made by the scientists at the Carmel Workshop on Cognitive Psychophysiology and Robert W. McCarley in their study and in publishing the article titled "Studies from Neuroscience Research Australia Update Current Data on Schizophrenia (Dysregulations of Synaptic Vesicle Trafficking in Schizophrenia). Robert W. McCarley writes:

> One can then compare the two groups on any number of measures, be it position emission tomography (PET), functional magnetic resonance imaging (fMRI), or ERPs, and cataloging the observed differences. The group was not persuaded that such an enterprise is particularly productive, because it leads to accumulation and cataloging of differences whose significance can rarely be placed in a useful theoretical context. Yet, such empirical explorations do sometimes yield serendipitous,

interesting observations and discoveries. Nonetheless, the group proceeded on the assumption that research should be based on theory.

The use of position emission tomography (PET) and functional magnetic resonance imaging (fMRI), or ERPs are used to set side by side two types of people who are meant to be divided and further separated by the use of the PET and fMRI, or ERP insofar as healthy neurological activity and neurology and dysregulations of synaptic vesicle trafficking in schizophrenia but the scientists at the Carmel Workshop of Cognitive Psychophysiology and Robert W. McCarley write that the accumulated data and catalogued differences in the neurologies of the two groups "can rarely be placed in a useful theoretical context" (McCarley). Furthermore, "such

empirical explorations do sometimes yield serendipitous, interesting observations and discoveries" (McCarley). It seems these scientists have a longing for eccentricity in discovering supposed "serendipitous" (McCarley) connections between otherwise non-parallel notions or data such as the daft correlation observed between PCP-mediated rates and the brains of the diagnosed schizophrenic. While these mental health professionals are filled with what they call intellectualism they have let escape them or have dismissed the very foundation of the scientific method and the foundations of existence which they are seeming to differentiate in the context of verbose individuals who are deviant in thought from a mental health professional point-of-view and speak their minds, or verbalize their thoughts.

LIFE AFTER SCHIZOPHRENIA

First, let us establish the reality of schizophrenia using Paul James's theory of existence before we establish its innate schismatic nature with the remaining logic we have. The definition of an epistemological existence is the embedded knowledge humanity has procured for itself. Epistemological is a term used to describe ideas like anthropology and culinary arts on a knowledge level basis. Anthropology and the culinary arts exists as typographical concepts and do in fact range across the span of all spheres of existence from the temporal sphere of existence to the performative sphere of existence which we shall define in little time. From an epistemological standpoint, yes, schizophrenia exists because it has a name and is an idea which is being development every single day; and schizophrenia is existent of the performative sphere of existence, too, for the reason and no other reason than its active role in sociological situations and the effects it has on interpersonal relations of those diagnosed with schizophrenia and those discussing schizophrenia. If schizophrenia were to be rated on a scale from one to five one being the lowest and most insubstantial quality of existence and five being the highest and most potent quality of existence schizophrenia would rate a two out of five for the remaining three spheres of existence are not identifiable nor do they house schizophrenia in any sense. Temporal existence is described as a bounding and rebounding scape that permeates throughout concrete reality via the time-space continuum or Albert Einstein's Brownian motion. Literature, theatre, visual art, tradition on a religious, spiritual, or familial level, and Charles Darwin's descent with modification through variation by natural selection, or the theory of evolution are examples of existence in the temporal sphere of existence. The above examples range through space and time and maintain a consistence throughout the changing world resilient and unmovable in a living world. Schizophrenia as a concept does not operate in the temporal sphere of existence for the reason that schizophrenia is a porous and translucent idea, or pane through which one can look to gain a view of a changing yet minuscule world. Schizophrenia is incomplete as a theory and as a concept and it is not reliable when viewed in conjunction with the temporal sphere of existence. To claim that schizophrenia exists on a spatial level would be an ugly idea to develop. To claim that schizophrenia exists on a spatial level would be to claim that schizophrenia had a body and traversed its way through corporeal existence (which will be defined below) and went to the grocery store to buy food, went to work and earned money, fed its children and significant other, drank and ate and thought and cleaned its living environment. To claim such a concept would be to claim that schizophrenia in all literalness embodied the individual and operated through them much like demonic possession. It is an uneducated, foolish, and ignorant claim and I do not think anybody with all their wits about them would make a claim as such. If one were to claim that schizophrenia existed in the spatial sphere of existence that individual who in all probability believed in schizophrenia as a whole would be quite incorrect. The corporeal sphere of existence and the spatial sphere of existence are close in relation. One cannot exist without the other. That schizophrenia does not exist in the spatial sphere of existence and does not have a material, or corporeal body with which to navigate and traverse existence is all the evidence the prognosticating and critical thinker needs to establish that schizophrenia does not exist in the corporeal sphere of existence. Only these five spheres of existence interacting simultaneous with one another can establish and prove the existence of a concept real and actual. There needs to be accordance with every sphere of existence for a concept to manifest in entirety. Hisaki states in his article "Phenomenon of Life and Death by Dōgen and Heidegger––In View of 'Embodied Cognition' in Buddhist Philosophy and Phenomenology":

> Moritz Schlick, who occupied a prominent position in the Vienna Circle, stated that the self, soul, psyche etc. which build up the metaphysical problem could be proved only by concrete positive, natural scientific facts, for example, in mutual communication and in the knowledge of persons in accordance (coherence) with the recognition of several data, A, B, C and so on. Under these conditions "acknowledging only the positive scientifically verifiable facts" is right, but there is something which has been neglected in this discourse of criticizing and omitting "idealism," "metaphysics," "religious intuition" etc.

Mental health professionals work in an ideal state of mind as far as they are concerned and metaphysics and religious intuition are nonexistent to them and are even used as preliminary points by which to claim the presence of and by which to move forward with the diagnosis of schizophrenia. Mental health professionals work on a foundation of neuroscience in the twenty first century and neglect the existence of such concepts as metaphysics and religious intuition and call them hallucinations and delusions. The dismissed metaphysical and religious intuitive notion roused in a candidate for the diagnosis schizophrenia are said, by both the mental health professional and the layman who believes the diagnosis schizophrenia, to be trauma in the brain and in the mind of the candidate for a diagnosis of schizophrenia, a trauma otherwise called brain damage. In fact, when that candidate for a diagnosis of schizophrenia claiming metaphysical contact or religious intuition walks into the psychologists' or psychiatrists' office the trauma has not yet become manifest. The trauma comes following the diagnosis of schizophrenia for reasons including the diagnoses' effects on the patients' social life, his or her position in the sociological hierarchy, and in familial exchanges and introspective meditations. Hisaki states in his article regarding embodied cognition that:

Physiologically, the overstimulated nerve in that part of the body transmits the information about a danger threatening in this situation as a series of electron signals from the damaged part to the central nerve system and to the cerebral cortex. This process is very fast, causing a drastic change in the mental and physical conditions. In psychic injury and trauma, this situation of subjectivity can be intensified: Only the person whose psyche was injured suffers his/her own trauma. If it is treated properly, the phenomenon of the trauma will become obsolete in the memory and vanish.

LIFE AFTER SCHIZOPHRENIA

It is my opinion, one which many believe to be factual, the symptoms typical of the diagnosed schizophrenic are of a psychic type. The fortification of schizophrenia in an individual's life and the implementation of treatments, medication and hospitalizations which follow a diagnosis of schizophrenia, are not ample means of proper treatment of a person with such psychic symptoms. In all idealism and counter to mental health professionals' theories of the ideal world, the ideal person or individual the illness should as Hisaki says in his article disappear and that in all idealism "the phenomenon of the trauma will become obsolete in the memory and vanish." The disappearance and vanishing of schizophrenia and its subsequent treatments in most individuals diagnosed with the disease let alone schizophrenia on a global scale seems, however, rather ideal at best and also has quite a bit of unlikeliness imbued with that idealism.

There is a hysterical circumvention within the mental health field at present. Individuals are being diagnosed with schizophrenia by mental health professionals with prematurity and the supposed causation of the mental disease is deviant brain chemistry, or brain damage. Mentalities, thoughts, ideas, and exchanges are not mathematical in nature at least not on any level I have heard of and I am quite confident in stating that scientists are working on cracking the mathematical, or for the lack of a better term binary sequence, or matrix of the human brain. For the time being, mentalities, thoughts, ideas, and exchanges are, as far as communication is concerned, ethereal and supple. In the case of mentalities, thoughts, ideas, and exchanges, the beginning of a notion and the end of the same notion is much like the dawn of life and the descending of death. The notion surfaces in thought, is toyed with, and escapes from mind. The ethereal thought forms which dictate our lives are not like mathematics.

There seems to be a dismissiveness on mental health professionals' parts when contending with individuals' deviant belief systems. The mental health professional claims the deviant belief system is an effect of deviant brain chemistry, or a neurological disorder. Hisaki states in his article: "Heidegger postulates that phenomenology is a method of investigation which shows itself openly, and which is obvious in itself. His phenomenology expresses a maxim, pointing 'to the things themselves!'" In so many words, the philosopher Heidegger claims that phenomenology or when discussing supposed schizophrenic phenomenon described as "florid psychotic symptoms of hallucinations and delusions" (McCarley) when attempting to ascertain the cause of phenomenon one must dig deep and find the cause of said phenomenon not only on a would-be corporeal sphere of existence, or neurological level but also on a temporal sphere of existence and all of the five spheres of existence in unison to achieve undeniable evidence that the phenomena, its cause, and its prevalence exist. Hisaki inquires:

> Is our existence in the world, as Heidegger asserts, a constant journey towards death in a finite series of "not yet" moments? Is death a termination of existence, and is being in life something incomplete? Heidegger discusses these problems and shows that

our existence is a "not yet" to death. For Heidegger, death is still beyond all phenomena; it has not yet been integrated into the problem of being.

Heidegger in Hisaki's article is questioning the existence of man as a whole and as an individual. Existential identification is not the point of this essay. Rather than addressing the issue of existence of man as a whole and as an individual I will address "the problem of being" (Hisaki) using the porous and translucent device of schizophrenia as a parallel to death and as the end of the former self and even the termination of the soul. The finite components of the self and of the soul will be discussed in the last essay in this book which is entitled "Schizophrenia and the Spiritual Nature of the Human." But, for now let us discuss the sovereign and self-actualizing notion that is schizophrenia. Connecting the two notions, death and schizophrenia, is simple to do when utilizing the elements of belief systems, phenomenology, and the concept of embodied cognition. Hisaki further states in his article that:

> Heidegger indicates a successive coming-into-being to arrive at the end; the impending death of our being. The problem of death (for Heidegger) is integrated into existence. Being thrown into the field of imminent death causes fear. Fear of death is integrated into being-in-the-world. Since the subject of fear is present even in our being-in-the-world, we might say: "Angst ängstet sich"/(fear fears itself).

The phrase used by Heidegger and Hisaki is much like the phrase used by President John F. Kennedy during his speech in Saginaw, Minnesota on 14 October 1960 and conveys the same meaning. One can make the parallel between the sovereign and self-actualizing phenomena that is schizophrenia and the ouroboros which is a symbol of a serpent pursuing and consuming its own tail. Schizophrenia is a perpetual phenomenon that feeds off of itself and takes residence in the incomplete belief systems on which it thrives. Schizophrenia is much like fear and schizophrenia is much like death. It takes hold once given the opportunity and does not let go until pried open and removed from an individual's life, and even then it will still be evident though not as obvious like an old scar from a snake bite. The excision of schizophrenia from the epistemological standpoint of an individual and the snubbing away of schizophrenia on a performative level, that is the rejection of the diagnosis as a whole and the acceptance of surfacing notions which may be metaphysical or religious intuition are the two essential foci in achieving a sense of self, greater and mightier than a former self. The internalization of fear, death, or schizophrenia—all three notions are the same and interchangeable—is the preliminary stage to the loss of soul. As stated, the definition of and source of the soul will be defined later in this book from the perspective of and using the fundamental key points of the modern theory of soul conceived by a well-known and timeless philosopher and psychologist named Carl Gustav Jung. The becoming of an individual and the opening of existence cannot be attained from a level on which the individual houses fear, death, or schizophrenia. The rejection of and resilience toward fear, death, and schizophrenia are the most important means and the most elementary means of achieving that which is the human mind's function and the meaning of life: variation.

Heidegger's theory regarding fear and death and illusion of self is a progenitor of the pansophic individual in a contemporary mental health universe. Hisaki writes:

> In his early works, such as Being and Time, he arrives at the conclusion that through encountering the void-ness of the existential Ab-grund, one tries to overcome existential 'fear' and creates the possibility of finally becoming oneself, primarily through 'an impassioned freedom towards death' having finally broken away from the illusions of self and factuality, whereas fear and anxiety could not be completely eliminated. He emphasizes the recognition of our being in a decisive view that this life is not necessarily independent of 'anxiety.' This position shows a confrontation with the dichotomy of life and death and a resolve to further that confrontation, in that one is to savor the depths of being, in contrast to its end and in the opening up of existence.

The enjoyment of a life and existence filled with carefree and unbiased individuals is an ideal setting for an existence in which we could all find ourselves in agreement and some would call such a setting with such carefree and unbiased individuals a utopian society. While utopia is a mythical and lofty height written on and provocated over many centuries it is not a realistic aspiration. For the time being, one must actualize who is the dominant individual in regards to the self and self-recognition and who is fearsome and who wields deadliness and what is schizophrenia; how do the fearsome and those who wield deadliness in the context of schizophrenia as death change an individual; how does schizophrenia and the mental health professional transport the introspective from one state of mind to another state of mind with the intention of altering a belief system. These inquiries can be solved and answered with ease. First, "an impassioned freedom towards death" (Hisaki) much be achieved and then can we address the issue of schizophrenia and its perpetuators in application.

Schizophrenia and its Devout Perpetuators

———

IT HAS BEEN ESTABLISHED that the psychological and psychiatric theatre through which mental health professionals and their patients work and reciprocate is schizophrenic in itself. One man or woman who is the patient resides in a polar opposite belief system as opposed to the mental health professionals who reside in a belief system which is common and accepted by society. It takes two individuals to make this scenario an item, or existent. One: the supposed mental ill who verbalizes a deviant thought; and two: the mental health professional whose intention it is to line up the patient with rational thoughts, to put the engine back on the tracks so to speak. Both individuals are needed to make schizophrenia an existent, albeit partial existence, and both individuals present make the notion schizophrenia immediate and rather fissured. In many cases the patient is brought to mental health professionals' domains not of their own accord. They are taken by friends or loved ones who deem their thoughts weird or unidentifiable. Then, the mental health professional takes his or her course of action and assumes the position of power, or dominance in that a premature decision, or rash misdiagnosis is made and can disturb and destroy an individual's life on a social, on an economic, and on an introspective, or spiritual level.

The mental health professional believes in full that schizophrenia is an existent, that is real and actual concept, while many men and women in danger of being donned this heinous association are having an existential, spiritual, or even religious awakening or heightened intuition.

Picking apart schizophrenia, or rather its devout perpetuators who believe in full that schizophrenia is a real and actual concept and can be used to describe an individual's intentions, conscious or unconscious, and his or her thoughts or ideas, is the intention of this essay and it will be done using the comprehensive characteristics of a belief system which total thirteen characteristics that make belief belief and speculation speculation.

The characteristics of a belief system work in synchronicity with one another and achieve a certain effect on society and the people and entities which compose society. All characteristics working in synchronicity with one another, creating together a belief system in an individual is called an ideology when the belief system takes on more individuals who identify with the belief system and when the belief system builds momentum. Uso-Domenech and Nescolarde-Selva write in their article "What are Belief Systems?" an effective and comprehensive definition of belief systems and ideologies. Uso-Domenech and Nescolarde-Selva define the first characteristic of a belief system as follows: "Personal commitment is one of most observable and interesting features of an ideology. If it were not for the fact of personal commitment, belief systems could not have strong social consequences, and the study of social systems would not be so interesting." Commitment insofar as a profession is good. Anybody will agree. But, the interesting term in the above definition for the first characteristic of a belief system is "ideology" which is defined as 1) a system of ideas and principles forming the basis of an economic or political theory, and 2) the set beliefs held by a social group: *bourgeois ideology*. Commitment, or persistence is a valuable and worthy trait in a professional but when having commitment, or persistence to the effect of manifesting a peripheral and ill social group, a group whose epistemological association is schizophrenia, the persistent mental health professional is widening the divide between social groups and resilience and confidence in their patient and are invoking in society as a whole schizophrenia.

The issue of motivation in the mental health professional and also in the patient who is verbalizing so called strange thoughts should be questioned and examined, too. Motivation is a two-fold, or dichotomous human trait. One type of motivation is intrinsic motivation. The other type of motivation is extrinsic motivation. It tends to be the case that when in the theatre of mental health and schizophrenia belief systems are at hand, what the patient claims to be experiencing, that is seeing floral phenomenon, hearing voices, and experiencing religious intuition, is real and believes it to be real while the mental health professional who resides in a belief system opposing the patient's belief system and who claims the floral phenomenon, the voices, and the religious intuition are hallucinations, delusions and fabricated, and hold no practical or applicable use in day to day life lean toward the opposite pole. When taking belief systems into account along with motivation, whether it be intrinsic or extrinsic and in a schizophrenic setting, pridefulness, too, is present and patients tend to get emotional, perhaps even violent and resentful as a result of mental health professionals' donning the patient with the diagnosis schizophrenia and disregarding the patient's thoughts and intuitions in full as neurological deviation. In such a case, commitment, persistence, and motivation on an intrinsic and extrinsic level can be catastrophic to the patient and to the family and friends of the patient for no other reason than a fissure in belief systems created and widened regarding floral phenomenon, auditory sensations which seem to come from the ether, and religious intuition.

Developing a belief system takes time. In the case of a mental health professional many years of schooling and curiosity take residence in the mental health professional and a belief system which fortifies the notion of schizophrenia becomes manifest. In those experiencing supposed unexplainable phenomena without the excuse, or scape goat that is neurological deviation the patient's belief system which differs from the mental health professional's belief system and which takes hold in spirituality and religiosity comes forth through manifold experiences that require a great deal of faith in the supernatural. It is misfortunate that the mental health professional has the same vigorous faith in mental disorder than the spiritual and religious advanced individuals who begin to verbalize their experiences have in the supernatural and metaphysical. As per sheer numbers and studies in neurological deviation and the vast rejection of god in the present age by many people who are in most cases scientists tend to outweigh the spiritual and religious advanced individuals' faiths. Instead of putting their faith in acceptance and compassion and good nature, people in many cases put their faith in money and science and athleticism.

Uso-Domenech and Nescolarde-Selva in regards to group polarization define the second characteristic of a belief system as follows: "Belief systems have an existence that is independent of their committed believers. The believers do not wholly contain the belief system; in fact, they are unlikely to be aware of more than a small part of it and, knowingly or unknowingly, they must take the rest of the belief system on faith." We have established the volatile possibilities of faith in the schizophrenic environment. Many people attempt to tamper with other individuals' belief systems and most are unsuccessful. Even in the schizophrenic environment the change in belief on the patient's end are in many cases not present, that is he or she misdiagnosed with schizophrenia still believes what they believed when first taken into the mental health professional's office but tell nobody about those beliefs anymore; now they just have the diagnosis schizophrenia to contend with for the remainder of their lives. A question arises when analyzing the belief systems and motivations, intrinsic and extrinsic, of an individual with the intention of wooing or coercing another into a separate belief system. The question is as follows: How and why does an individual take such an active role in the influencing of another as far as beliefs? It is a simple question which can be answered in many ways, from a subconscious staging point, from a pridefulness perspective, and from a philosophical point-of-view. For all intents and purposes, the question is answered with definitiveness by Uso-Domenech and Nescolarde-Selva in their article. The answer is as follows:

> Confronted with a conflict between evidence and what they want to believe for political and/or religious reasons, many people reject the evidence. And knowing more about the issues widen the divide, because the well-informed have a clearer view of which evidence they need to reject to sustain their belief system.

The answer in short is sustainability, or longevity of a person and his or her belief systems and the preservation of a foundational foothold on which one's entire life was built. In the case of the mental health professional the existence of schizophrenia is needed. From the perspective of the spiritual and religious advanced individual the belief in macrocosmic nature, or metaphysics and its omnipresence is necessary for introspection and personal development. The projection of schizophrenia onto the latter of the two individuals above dampens the spirituality, religiosity, and internal growth of the patient whether the patient knows or not what they are experiencing is spiritual, religious, or introspective.

A device usable to exhibit the erroneous faith of many people in the contemporary world is the dollar and the faith propagated behind it and used to further its seeming value. The number of U.S. legal tenders circulating throughout the planet earth leaves me incredulous and unbelieving that the banknotes still hold value outside of collective faith in them.

LIFE AFTER SCHIZOPHRENIA

What else would the individual, a man or woman need to buy a gallon of whole milk from the convenience store for their child or a bar of soap from the pharmacy to wash? What else would a child need to extract a gum ball from a gum ball machine without the use of anarchy, or destructiveness? The answer as far as the twenty-first century is concerned is quite blatant when opening your wallet to find three or four credit cards reaching their limit for the present month. Currency now is transposed electronic through the non-space of political and socio-economic power and is backed by a mixed faith and fear. Currency holds no weight outside of the fists of a mugger or the red hands of a thief. For that reason the free market and the faithful are quite disembodied and in danger. Krugman writes in his article titled "Faith vs. facts when it comes to monetary policy" that, "On the eve of the Great Recession, many conservative pundits and commentators—and quite a few economists—had a worldview that combined faith in free markets with disdain for government." The fact of life is one cannot have one without the other. One cannot have free markets without the government. They are two sides of the same coin. One comes with the other much like deviating belief systems and schizophrenia. Krugman goes on to write in his article, "Also, let's not forget that quite a few influential conservatives, including Mr. Ryan, draw their inspiration from Ayn Rand novels in which the gold standard takes on essentially sacred status." The combined faith in money has elevated the perspective of monetary policy to sacredness like Ayn Rand had predicted making her a prophet. The combined and collective faith in mental disorder is much like Ayn Rand's prophesying the holy dollar only the faith and collective belief system which keeps the seeming unconquerable tower of schizophrenia erect like scaffolding is harnessed and utilized to shift individual's belief systems which are as Krugman states in his article in regards to the status of the gold standard sacred in their source and remains arguable in their prescience. Krugman finishes his article with a timeless and true statement which is the case relevant to all belief systems: "When faith—including faith-based economics—meets evidence, evidence doesn't stand a chance." Krugman states the faith of the consumer in the economy is stronger than and outweighs the evidence regarding the devaluing of global monetary policy much like I have stated the collective faith of the mental health professional outweighs the dying belief systems of the spiritual and religious advanced individual under examination by the mental health professional.

The human mind makes use of many mechanisms to bolster a belief system. One has been established in the above paragraphs, that is the use of rejection of evidence which negates another's belief system in order to fortify one's own belief system which already exists and is questionable. Another innate mechanism used by the human mind to fortify pre-existing belief systems is the third characteristic of a belief system: "Psychological mechanisms such as cognitive congruence may help explain individual commitment, but they do not necessarily explain the connectedness of a belief system in human society." The term cognitive congruence is the briefest way to convey the third characteristic of a belief system and is defined as a type of cognitive bias similar to confirmation bias. Cognitive congruence bias occurs due to people's over reliance on directly testing a given hypothesis as well as neglecting indirect testing. In so many words, people are plugging in the missing parts of an equation with evidence that is usable and applicable to the hypothesis undergoing testing. That is scientists when studying schizophrenia find gaps in their theory and fill the gaps with notions such as dysfunction in the neurological synapses and make parallels such as the misfortunate documentation regarding the PCP-mediated rat in conjunction with the brain chemistry of one diagnosed with schizophrenia to found a valid claim, or supposed evident relation between the ethereal theory of schizophrenia and actual existence. To evoke an image in this rather illogical chain of events which is all too the case in contemporary science and research one can impose and make a parallel between the incomplete, shoddy workmanship of the scientist and the mental health professional with gestalt psychology. Gestalt psychology was founded by Max Wertheimer in 1912 and was to some extent a rebellion against the molecularism of Wundt's program for psychology. The word gestalt means a unified or meaningful whole and was to be the focus of psychological study instead of a molecular, or microcosmic point-of-view. In an article titled "A Century of Gestalt Psychology in Visual Perception: I. Perceptual Grouping and Figure–ground Organization" published in *Psychological Bulletin* it is written that:

> For von Ehrenfels, Gestalt qualities rest unidirectionally on sense data: Wholes are more than the sums of their parts, but the parts are the foundation of the whole. In contrast, Wertheimer

claimed that functional relations determine what will appear as the whole and what will appear as parts (i.e., reciprocal dependency). Often the whole is grasped even before the individual parts enter consciousness. (Wagemans)

Wertheimer's claim that the human mind completes the incomplete without intention and as a part of its nature is the same mindful device used to ground the theory of schizophrenia in the psychological and psychiatric fields of study. That is to say, the unexplainable is explained and the unnatural is made natural by the only means available to the mental health professional and their bias judgment regarding so called hallucinations and delusions and the seeming correlation between chemical imbalances in the brain and claims made by those misdiagnosed with schizophrenia. Gestalt psychology was implemented on many different levels of the human being from pure visual sensations and geometric continuity to social connectivity like political regimes and fields of science like Nazi Germany and zoology. To superimpose, or evoke an image which can relate to the seeming disconnectedness of schizophrenic culture one can examine a study made by Wertheimer in regards to optical continuity provoked by the human mind's innate longing for sensical and complete ideas. Wagemans writes:

Max Wertheimer first posed the problem of perceptual grouping in his groundbreaking 1923 paper by asking what stimulus factors influence the perceived grouping of discrete elements. He first demonstrated that equally spaced dots do not group together into larger perceptual units, except as a uniform line, and then noted that when he altered the spacing between adjacent dots so that some dots were closer than others, the closer ones grouped together strongly into pairs. This factor of relative distance, which Wertheimer called proximity, was the first of his famous laws or (more accurately) principles of grouping.

If this optical representation of the surfacing and perpetuation of schizophrenia as a theory and belief system is not in semblance with each other I do not know what could be a better symbol in all effectiveness. That gestalt and visual theoretical sensations insofar as the spatial sphere of existence holds true Wertheimer's studies of geometry, line segments, and dots on a line and their seeming relation to one another makes a candid representation of the political and socio-economic, familial and patient-mental health professional's movements in contemporary perception. That is to say:

> As shown by Maxwell and Planck, all processes in physical systems, left to themselves, show a tendency to achieve the maximal level of stability (homogeneity, simplicity, symmetry) with the minimum expenditure of energy allowed by the prevailing conditions. More specific principles that determine perceptual organization according to Wertheimer were proximity, similarity, uniform

density, common fate, direction, good continuation
and whole properties (or Ganzeigenschaften) such
as closure, equilibrium, and symmetry.

While terms used by Wertheimer like "proximity," "uniform
destiny," "common fate," and "good continuation" were meant
to be regarded on a simple, X-Y, two-dimensional axis, or plane
the terms can very well be applied to communication and
interpersonal relation and with especial prominence in the
mental health professional's office. An individual with a belief
system that differs with such greatness from another's belief
system such as an advanced individual who is having psionic
or metaphysical experiences and believes it is not a problem
nor a mental or neurological deviation and the mental health
professional's belief system which judges the supposed
symptoms as incompetence and assumes they are unhealthy
is bound to be molested as per Wertheimer's "proximity" and
"uniform destiny." That is the misfortunate individuals who
have just been hit with a misdiagnosis of schizophrenia are
collected and perceived as one type of person is an instant
of "common fate" and "good continuation." This is an instant
that is becoming far too prevalent and is a trend that has been
picking up momentum since the turn of the millennium.
While ignorant of the foundations of psychology and
humanity it is nevertheless all too the case.

Gestalt psychologists in the early twentieth century found that
individuals in a "civilized" society next to those from a savage,
tribalistic society differed in a great many ways when regarding
"good continuation" in that the "civilized" peoples perceived
completed triangles when the triangles were not in fact

complete and those in savage, or tribalistic societies claimed not to see a triangle but three non-linear line segments. One is apt to think how civilization and the manipulation of existence is at hand in conjunction with savage, or tribalistic societies. The civilized man is prone to adaptations of existence which are composed of categorizations and hierarchies and which differ from those of savage, or tribalistic societies who operate from a holistic point-of-view and who experience supposed mental health issues on a minimal level, if at all as per the absence of its invention and the placement of faith in a more spiritual and religious locale. In this regard, the two peoples' psychological adaptations of existence differ with greatness. Who is to say one people's psychological adaptation, or belief system is healthier than another people's psychological adaptation, or belief system? All men and women on the planet earth live and die within a certain number of years. All men and women albeit not victim to tragedy or sickness live to see about sixty to eighty years of age. But, that is not to say those individuals' belief systems die, or perish along with the individuals themselves. In fact, their psychological adaptations, or belief systems live for a far longer period of time than the individuals themselves who have claimed those psychological adaptations, or belief systems.

Another characteristic of a belief system which can be intuited with ease at this point is the following and fifth characteristic of a belief system: "Belief systems vary almost infinitely in substantive content." That is to say, belief systems are not grounded, or constant. They are always changing, oscillating, and developing. Substantive content in the context of the above characteristic of a belief system is defined as content which is unquestionable in regards to existence like the effects of caffeine or the first amendment of the Constitution of the United States of America. This characteristic in its almost infinite interpretations in regards to constant, or granted substantive content is in good conjunction with the following characteristic of a belief system: "The boundaries of a belief system are generally, although not always, undefined. Collections of beliefs do not generally have neat boundaries." This aspect of a belief system and its stating that belief systems lack neat boundaries is a precise mark in the separation of belief systems regarding schizophrenia and for the lack of a better term schizophrenic symptoms. While schizophrenia exists on a minute, or partial level the boundaries which keep it thriving and developing as a theory, or belief system is a no man's land of baseless faith and is viscous at best. The topic of schizophrenia is a theory, or concept which will forever be disagreed upon. This sort of topic is unworthy of study from a scientific standpoint. By all means philosophize on the mind from a humanistic standpoint but the attempt to ground, or tether a translucent theory like schizophrenia to a populace is rather unwise, vain, and even juvenile. What makes the topic of schizophrenia so sensitive is the commingling of the topic schizophrenia as a knowledge system and as a belief system. The seventh characteristic and one which applies to the patient in a given mental health professional scenario is as follows:

> The elements (concepts, propositions, rules, etc.) of belief systems are not consensual. That is, the elements of one system might be quite different

from those of a second in the same content domain. And a third system may be different from each. Individual differences of this kind do not generally characterize ordinary knowledge systems, except insofar as one might want to represent differences in capability or complexity. Belief systems may also vary in complexity, but the most distinctive variation is conceptual variation at a roughly comparable level of complexity. An interesting sidelight on the consensuality question is whether a belief system is "aware," in some sense, that alternative constructions are possible. For cognitive science, the point of this discussion is that nonconsensuality should somehow be exploited if belief systems are to be interesting in their own right as opposed to knowledge systems. Belief systems often appear to have clear boundaries when the separation is really between social groups. (Uso-Domenech and Nescolarde-Selva)

Speaking of belief in regards to a supposed medical diagnosis to the imperceptive may seem rather foolish, or inconsequential. But, the fact remains that there is a discrepancy between what the patient believes exists as real or actual regarding so called hallucinations or delusions and what the mental health professional believes exists as real or actual in regards to healthiness. It is difficult if not impossible to distinguish what is existent when dealing with the supernatural or metaphysical, the spiritual and religious and most difficult in a mental health professional setting. So called symptoms range in intensity and type from auditory whispers to bold declarations heard only by the supernatural or metaphysical, spiritual and religious aware to ear shattering shrieks at any given time of day. Symptoms range from optical anomalies to past and future precognition and retrocognition. Some patients claim these experiences are existent and believe in their prescience but the verbose, or misfortunate who tend to lose composure under such intense sensations and perceptions are placed under a generalized and consensual, or socionormative perception of these experiences by the mental health professional and in some cases friends and family alike and are known as schizophrenic. At the point of diagnosis one factor comes into play which is quite pressurized and scrutinized: the patient's functionality, or behavior. The rejection of a patient's belief systems can and does do much harm in terms of his or her metaphysical wellbeing, spirituality, religiosity, and introspectiveness in terms of causality on people and environments and in terms of his or her metaphysical, spiritual, religious, and interpersonal nature in the future regarding effectuality on individuals and social settings.

The characteristics of a belief system as written by Uso-Domenech and Nescolarde-Selva who did not have the theory of schizophrenia in mind when writing their article listing and expounding on the characteristics of a belief system are rather well set in the continual and debatable topic of the theory of schizophrenia. All of the above seven characteristics delineate, or separate existing belief systems regarding schizophrenia from a logical and prognosticated level and not from absolute passion. The eighth characteristic of a belief system is a good stand point from which to scrutinize the basis of the theory schizophrenia, so called hallucinations and delusions. It reads:

> Belief systems are in part concerned with the existence or nonexistence of certain conceptual entities. God, motherland, witches, and assassination conspiracies are examples of such entities. This feature of belief systems is essentially a special case of the nonconsensuality feature. To insist that some entity exists implies an awareness of others who believe it does not exist. Moreover, these entities are usually central organizing categories in the belief system, and as such, they may play an unusual role which is not typically to be found in the concepts of straightforward knowledge systems. (Uso-Domenech and Nescolarde-Selva)

This characteristic which is the foundation of skepticism in the supernatural, the metaphysical, the spiritual, and the religious will recur as far as theme and types of so called psychotic breaks from reality in the fifth and final essay in this book titled "Schizophrenia and the Spiritual Nature of the Human." The essential gist of both this characteristic and the similar breaking down of the three types of psychotic breaks from reality which will be located in the fifth essay establishes, or declares that for a belief system to be in fact a belief system there must be two opposing, or polar opposite groups of people which border on either side the belief system, on one side those believing in, as the above characteristic suggests, an "entity" and on the other side of the belief system the group of people who do not believe in the "entity" in question. Furthermore, the characteristic above states that in most cases the side which houses those believing in the "entity" is countered by those who believe in a straightforward knowledge system which to be frank insofar as the theory of schizophrenia is concerned is rather hypocritical based on the passionate decisions and gestaltan psychologies of the mental health professional. While not all belief systems, such as the moon landing hoax or the Loch Ness monster, are as chastised as voices being heard from seeming ether or strange optical phenomenon or intuition which seems rather illogical and has been voiced there is always a basis, or cause and one might even declare the cause corporeal or material to such claims and cannot be disregarded or dismissed without ignorance. In most cases the dose of ignorance which goes along with the dismissal of otherworldly claims is quite substantial.

It can be said that the mental health professional is longing for an ideal, or utopian world in which all individuals are purged of what the mental health professional considers ill or baseless when regarding belief systems. This utopian idealism is the very trait in the mental health professional which deems him or her self-righteous and intrusive although this may not be known to them. The attempt made by the mental health professional to redirect one's thoughts, belief systems, and in effect society as a whole in many cases backfires and the attempt to redirect one's thoughts, belief systems, et cetera whether a success or failure leaves all involved rather cut short of a naturalistic, or homeostatic coming of age. Characteristic nine reads:

LIFE AFTER SCHIZOPHRENIA

Belief systems often include representations of alternative worlds, typically the world as it is and the world as it should be. Revolutionary or Utopian belief systems especially have this character. The world must be changed in order to achieve an idealized state, and discussions of such change must elaborate how present reality operates deficiently, and what political, economic, social (etc.) factors must be manipulated in order to eliminate the deficiencies.   (Uso-Domenech   and Nescolarde-Selva)

In this regard the mental health professional is more radical than the so called psychotic individual. If the mental health professional is desiring an ideal, utopian society comprised of individuals who are healthy in mentality and in physicality the alienation of people including but not limited to the schizophrenic has backfired and not on an individualistic basis but on a societal basis, political basis, and economic basis. In a societal sense, one diagnosed with schizophrenia must deal with assumptions, or preconceived notions regarding a diagnosis, or misdiagnosis of schizophrenia that leaves the assumer questioning the so called schizophrenic individual's integrity and worthiness from a level which cannot be separated from potential violence. On a political level nations are chastised, or tainted with a reputation of a large populace of those with mental illness, Australia, Sweden, and the United States of America among the most misfortunate regarding this association. On an economic level those diagnosed with schizophrenia must contend with medications and psychological treatment which get into the tens of thousands of dollars per year as per cost of psychotropic and psychological treatment, an aspect that most individuals diagnosed with schizophrenia believe is necessary with which to contend for good functionality and behavior in society and an aspect which I will expound upon in the essay "Schizophrenia: the Green, the Guilty, and the Bamboozled" which gets into the incredible amounts of money collected by the pharmaceutical industry. As said in characteristic four of a belief system, "Believers are ephemeral, have means to change surroundings" (Uso-Domenech and Nescolarde-Selva). But, the way politics, economics, and society are perpetuating now, the change being made as far as the mental health industry as a whole is not ideal though professionals tend to expedite the trend at hand indiscriminate of other, peripheral belief systems or options available. I will not get into the other ways in which individuals could attain better medical treatment and medication if necessary because it would entail an entire book in itself to convey with clarity. Instead, I will continue on the evaluative and affective components of a belief system and the bias perceptions of "good" and "bad" cognitive categories. Characteristic ten reads as follows and is a lens through which to look at "good" versus "bad" and morality from a historical level. Characteristic ten of a belief system reads:

> Belief systems rely heavily on evaluative and affective components. There are two aspects to this, one "cognitive"; the other "motivational." Belief systems typically have large categories of concepts defined in one way or another as themselves "good"

or "bad," or as leading to good or bad outcomes. These polarities, which exert a strong organizing influence on other concepts within the system, may have a very dense network of connections, rare in ordinary knowledge systems. From a formal point of view, however, the concepts of "good" and "bad" might for all intents and purposes be treated as cold cognitive categories, just like any other categories of a knowledge system. (Uso-Domenech and Nescolarde-Selva)

We have established the discrepancy between the perceptions of so called schizophrenic symptoms as good versus bad and I will not continue on that subject. Instead, an individual who was revolutionary and considered rather mad and psychotic at the time of his studies and too deemed heretical from a religious standpoint was Galileo Galilei who made groundbreaking observations regarding astronomy in the early seventeenth century. Among his most groundbreaking discoveries are the observable phases of Venus, the detection of the four largest satellite moons of Jupiter named the Galilean moons after the astronomer, the observation and analysis of sunspots, and the deduction of a now universal belief called heliocentrism all with an archaic telescope, archaic at least from man's own contemporary conception of the telescope. Galileo Galilei had made an enemy as per his writings regarding the heavens and heliocentrism and that enemy was Pope Paul V who requested a meeting following the publication of Galileo Galilei's Copernican writings so the astronomer could defend his writings and the claims they suggested. Throughout the trial Galileo Galilei denied Copernican ideology which is the basis of the theory heliocentrism even while being threatened with torture if found to be lying about his Copernican affiliation. On 22 June 1633, the verdict and sentence was given by which Galileo Galilei would have to abide until 8 January 1642, the date of his death. The verdict and sentence was divided into three parts:

(1) Galileo Galilei was found "vehemently suspect to heresy" insofar as his claim that the sun remained motionless at the center of the universe and that the earth is not its center and moves, circling the sun after it had been declared contrary to holy scripture.

2) Galileo Galilei was forced into house arrest at the pleasure of the Inquisition. The day following the termination of the trial Galileo Galilei was to be confined within his home for the duration of his life.

3) His publication in question, *Dialogue*, was banned as was all Galileo Galilei's other works. All additional work was to remain unpublished. His future works were not to see the light of day.

The delineation in these belief systems, one being the disbelief of heliocentrism by the Catholic church and the other being heliocentrism's apparent prevalence, is a worthy and most relevant theatre through which to examine the difference between "good" and "bad" cognitive categories and the bias nature of what the tenth characteristic of a belief system states is the culprit of such miscommunication: a dense network of connections. Higher thinking as is the case of Galileo Galilei is similar to the higher thinking put forth in this essay regarding the so called schizophrenic experiences such as the auditory, optical, and temporal sensations and perceptions many call psychosis, or a psychotic break from reality. The congested, dense network of connections evident in familial, societal, and mental health professional settings when in disagreement about the application and practicality and the existence of such phantasmagoria can impede or diminish empathy which is essential to interpersonal and introspective development as per the belief in disorder rather than order. The "good" and the "bad," morality and immorality are subjective in most cases and can be called cold cognitive categories. While "good," "bad," morality, and immorality are subjective in most cases I do not state as a deduction, or interpretation of this book that mental deviation does not exist. The beginning of all public shootings in Columbine, Colorado and a most recent shooting in a nightclub in Orlando, Florida are proof of mental deviation which had fatal outcomes.

Looking at schizophrenia from the overall perception of the schizophrenic individual in context with the above fatal instances is rather unnecessary and pointless. Schizophrenia tends to be a blanket which is thrown over the populous who has a set, or fixed perceptive set and who share functionary or behavioral issues. While not all so called symptoms are nor should they be classified as psychotic symptoms some symptoms like functionary or behavioral issues should and are classified as psychotic symptoms. The requisites, however, for deviant functionary or behavioral issues ought to be considered in the context of the psychotic individual's societal background and familial exchanges which may be deemed unorthodox. Characteristic eleven of a belief system reads as follows: "Belief systems are likely to include a substantial amount of episodic material from either personal experience or (for cultural belief systems) from folklore or (for political doctrines) from propaganda" (Uso-Domenech and Nescolarde-Selva). This characteristic of a belief system tends to skew the causality and effectuality when regarding schizophrenia in the present era. As stated many public massacres have occurred and have been casted over with a term, or association to schizophrenia which is a blatant instant of the usage and implementation of gestalt psychology, or as a means to rationalize the heinous occurrences with something understandable and identifiable. Public killings are legitimized by the running together of schizophrenia and irrationality, or thoughtless murder in the cases of the two public shootings above.

The Florida State University, too, has had its exchange with the rather spontaneous and anomalous occurrence known as a public shooting. One individual walked into the Strozier library on the Florida State University campus and fired his gun a few times not killing anybody but injuring some and putting the reputation and perception of a generation and by association all those affected by mental health issues in danger. Most of those affected by the diagnosis schizophrenia and other mental health diagnoses are as opposed to these murderous individuals functional and peaceful and well-composed. The cause and effect, that is the violent behavior and the diagnoses are in fact mixed up, or juxtaposed. The identities of the shooters in these instances and the identities of the misdiagnosed are called into question when such a hasty and ignorant miscommunication or correlation is made.

As the twelfth characteristic of a belief system states an individual is not composed of nor carries an identity flagged by a belief system. This goes for the patient and mental health professional alike. In fact,

> The content set to be included in a belief system is usually highly "open." That is, it is unclear where to draw a boundary around the belief system, excluding irrelevant concepts lying outside. This is especially true if personal episodic material is important in the system. Consider, for example, a parental belief system about the irresponsibility and ingratitude of the modern generation of youth. Suppose, as might very well be the case, that central to this system is a series of hurtful episodes involving the believer's own children. For these episodes to be intelligible, it would be necessary for the system to contain information about these particular children, about their habits, their development, their friends, where the family lived at the time, and so on. And one would have to have similar conceptual amplification about the "self" of the believer. (Uso-Domenech and Nescolarde-Selva)

ANDERS M. SVENNING

It is stated in the twelfth characteristic of a belief system that the essential components of an irresponsible or ingratiating individual are "their habits, their development, their friends, where the family lived at the time [of the behavioral deviation or supposed psychotic break from reality], and so on" (Uso-Domenech and Nescolarde-Selva). These components from habits to the location of a family's home at the time of the behavioral deviation or supposed psychotic break from reality applies to the mental health professional and his or her belief systems too when taking into account "their habits, their development, their friends, where the family lived at the time [of the acquisition of their education and belief systems regarding mental health and also at the time of their dispensing of the diagnosis schizophrenia upon metaphysical and supernatural, spiritual and religious aware individuals], and so on." In all cases the identity of an individual is from a macrocosmic perspective based on and enlarged by a societal perspective, from family and friends, from doctors (psychological, psychiatric, physical, and any other doctor alike), political affiliation, citizenry, ethnicity, musical and artistic and sexual preferences, religiosity, and even inclinations regarding taste and cuisine. It tends to be the case that this eclectic and diverse society tends for some to have within its creases some detritus which makes the acceptance of any or all of above titular aspects of identities unlikable or unfavorable when taking into account one's own titular aspects of identity. This is most the case in those claiming deviant thoughts as per associations which have been made and which have been fortified by the uneducated and by our retaliating society, retaliating from abrasive or as the twelfth characteristic of a belief system states "hurtful episodes" (Uso-Domenech and Nescolarde-Selva).

The final characteristic of a belief system is the thirteenth which states that belief systems are enamored with an innate variation when taking into account certitude of a theory, or an idea in question. This variation as the thirteenth characteristic of a belief system states is absent in knowledge systems. The thirteen characteristic of a belief system reads:

> Beliefs can be held with varying degrees of certitude. The believer can be passionately committed to a point of view, or at the other extreme could regard a state of affairs as more probable than not. This dimension of variation is absent from knowledge systems. One would not say that one knew a fact strongly. There exists some examples of attempts to model variable credences or "confidence weights" of beliefs and how these change as a function of new information. A distinction should be made between the certitude attaching to a single belief and the strength of attachment to a large system of beliefs. (Uso-Domenech and Nescolarde-Selva)

Also stated in the thirteenth characteristic of a belief system is the evident "variable credences or 'confidence weights'" (Uso-Domenech and Nescolarde-Selva) which for all intents and purposes when dealing with schizophrenia and ethereal thought forms are the patients themselves. Functionality of an individual comes into play when examining the validity of the theory of schizophrenia in conjunction with the separate and vast variations of functionality in the schizophrenic populace. The generalization of temporary ineptitude or dysfunctionality which has been made by the mental health professional and the patient's family and friends and the rejection of other knowledge domains does open possibilities to the dismantlement of the broad diagnosis schizophrenia and even the criminalistic mental health industry. The dismissiveness of the mental health professional and all who maintain this faulty belief system and misplacement of faith enact the removal of the human element known as freewill which will be defined below using the device known as the elements of belief systems.

As opposed to the characteristics of belief systems which are the effects of a belief system after it has taken hold on an individual and populace the elements of a belief system are the rudiments, or ingredients of a belief system before it takes hold, when the individual is still in infancy in regards to intellectualism. The following elements are listed in the order that is logical and required for the understanding of a belief system. The order of the elements of belief systems does not imply priority in value nor does it imply priority in causal or historical senses. Many of the elements are quite similar to the characteristics of belief systems so I will cover them with quickness. The first element of belief systems:

> Values Implicitly or Explicitly, belief systems define what is good or valuable. Ideal values tend to be abstract summaries of the behavioral attributes which social system rewards, formulated after the fact. Social groups think of themselves, however, as

setting out various things in order to implement their values. Values are perceived as a priori, when they are in fact a posteriori to action. Having abstracted an ideal value from social experience, a social group may then reverse the process by deriving a new course of action from the principle. At the collective level of social structure, this is analogous to the capacity for abstract thought in individual subjects and allows great (or not) flexibility in adapting to events. Concrete belief systems often substitute observable social events for the immeasurable abstract ideal values to give the values immediate social utility.

This is the same basic idea as stated above concerning value systems, idealism, and utopian society. Idealism or utopia is a concept or setting which has no concern for scarcity on any level as per the infinite abundance of what is considered a value. As stated in the first element of belief systems "values are perceived as a priori, when they are in fact a posteriori to action" (Uso-Domenech and Nescolarde-Selva), an idea which may need some clarification as far as the definitions of the terms priori and posteriori. A priori knowledge or justification is independent of experience as with mathematics. There is no arguing that when one has one avocado and the other has one avocado there are two avocados. There is no arguing that there are two avocados unless one of the two people in the above scenario is known to be a pathological liar which would be an example of posteriori knowledge or justification i.e. a value or unit of knowledge dependent on experience or empirical (or societal) evidence as with personal knowledge.

When regarding schizophrenia and the mental health professional and industry the first element of belief system goes on to state, "Having abstracted an ideal value from social experience, a social group may then reverse the process by deriving a new course of action from the principle," (Uso-Domenech and Nescolarde-Selva) which is yet another instance of gestalt psychology, or the implementation of rationalization to achieve a threshold or discover a route toward the longed for flawlessness of utopia. The social group "having abstracted an ideal value from social experience" (Uso-Domenech and Nescolarde-Selva), reversing the process and changing the course of action of their subjects' lives, is the mental health professional who conflicts in belief systems with his or her subjects, disregards their intentions, and dismisses their belief systems as nonexistent and as symptoms of mental illness, removing human and homeostatic freewill.

The second element of belief systems:

> Substantive Beliefs (Sb), They are the more important and basic beliefs of a belief system. Statements such as: all the power for the people, God exists, Black is Beautiful, and so on, comprise the actual content of the belief systems and may take almost any form. For the believers, substantive beliefs are the focus of interest. (Uso-Domenech and Nescolarde-Selva)

LIFE AFTER SCHIZOPHRENIA

There are no clichés for schizophrenia that I know of. If there were I am sure they would be deprecating to the group of people with the misfortunate diagnosis. Substantive beliefs, however, are the rudimentary notions that evolve into larger political, economic, and societal actions and play into the third element of belief systems known as "orientation," an action which concludes with the coining of the name of a theory, or belief system and fabrication of the theory, or belief system (in this case schizophrenia) as a notion. The third element of belief systems reads:

> Orientation, The believer may assume the existence of a framework of assumptions around his thought. It may not actually exist. The orientation he shares with other believers may be illusory. For example, consider almost any politic and sociologic belief system. Such a system evolves highly detailed and highly systematic doctrines long after they come into existence and they came into existence for rather specific substantive beliefs. Believers interact, share specific consensuses, and give themselves a specific name: Marxism, socialism, Nazism, etc. Then, professionals of this belief system work out an orientation, logic, sets of criteria of validity, and so forth. (Uso-Domenech and Nescolarde-Selva)

Schizophrenia was invented and implemented in society from the date 24 April 1908 by an individual named Paul Eugen Blueler at a lecture at a meeting of the German Psychiatric Association in Berlin on the basis that dementia præcox, the name used for vague and various mental deviations before the invention and implementation of the theory and term schizophrenia, was terminal in the sense of further progression of mental health theory and was not apt for further adjectives of substantives. A quote from Paul Eugen Blueler's speech given on 24 April 1908 at the German Psychiatric Association in Berlin, the quote which brought the theory, or term schizophrenia to the surface of society and science reads as follows:

> "For the sake of further discussion I wish to emphasize that in Kraepelin's dementia præcox it is neither a question of an essential dementia nor of a necessary precociousness. For this reason, and because from the expression dementia præcox one cannot form further adjectives nor substantives, I am taking the liberty of employing the word schizophrenia for revising the Kraepelinian concept. In my opinion, the breaking up or splitting of psychic functioning is an excellent symptom of the whole group."

Paul Eugen Blueler takes the liberty in this quote to assume leadership on a vessel which he did not know would be compelled with such ferocity into the twenty-first century and which he did not know would change the face of existence on many levels. Following the delivering of his speech to the German Psychiatric Association in Berlin the path was cleared for the mental health professional and advancements in a field of study which are dissociated in their entirety, taking into account the criterion needed for an individual to be donned a so called schizophrenic individual. Paul Eugen Blueler states that dementia præcox as a study was vague and in its criterion various. The coining of schizophrenia as a term and its implementation in society and in the scientific world is redundant when taking its forefather, dementia præcox, into account as per the omnipresent vagueness and variousness in its studies and criterion coalescing around present day schizophrenia.

By accommodating himself to the spatial and temporal environment of his patients, [Blueler] realized that the condition was not a single disease (he referred to a "whole group" of schizophrenias), was not invariably incurable, and did not always progress to full dementia, nor did it always and only occur in young people. (Fusar-Poli)

Observation of schizophrenic patients made by Paul Eugen Blueler in regards to their spatial and temporal environment as the above quote suggests is a moot point and a meek point at best. Spatial and temporal environments are null and void when using a mental health device through which to observe patients; this is the case for no other reason than the patients' environment, actions and interactions, and conversations with the mental health professional performing the observation while residing in that length of time in a microcosm which is not at all a valid representation of existence and which is called a mental institution. The containment and observation of so called mental ill patients and the misdiagnosed schizophrenic is unjust. But, I do not speak only from a civil liberties standpoint. I speak from a scientific and professional standpoint, too, science and professionalism being a supposed empirical study and rather ignorant when being practiced in a confined, encapsulated setting in a mental health theatre when those being observed are being analyzed insofar as societal functionality.

If one were to base scientific observations and make assumptions using a microcosmic theatre such as a mental institution one could look into the world famous Philip Zimbardo social psychology study, the Stanford Prison Experiment (SPE). This study has been solidified in psychology record books as a valuable and valid thesis on social psychology in a prison system, or microcosm, the power hungriness of those in a position of authority and mirthful emasculation, and the problem of role-playing individuals and obedience in a sadistic environment. Bottoms writes in his article titled "Timeless Cruelty: Performing the Stanford Prison Experiment":

> Turning the clock back to 1971—a key year in the evolution of performance art—the following discussion examines one of the classic case studies in social psychology, Philip Zimbardo's Stanford Prison Experiment (SPE). This 'constructed situation' involved young, male volunteers being cast in the dichotomized roles of guard and prisoner in a simulated prison environment, to test their responses to role and circumstance. Traditionally,

the experiment's findings have been treated, not least by Zimbardo himself, as demonstrating 'timeless' scientific truths.

Many are familiar with the Philip Zimbardo Stanford Prison Experiment. It is one of the most famous, timeless, and true psychological experiments ever administered as per the interchangeability of the prison setting which Philip Zimbardo employed for his experiment with any other corporeal or temporal prison present in society as we know it, be it poverty, or ghettoization, supposed feminine roles in the home and workplace, or codependence in regards to the millennial youth and the hysterical yearning for ivory tower status. Those familiar with the Philip Zimbardo Stanford Prison Experiment may know that the experiment was cut short due to "extreme emotional depression, crying, rage, and acute anxiety...[and] psychosomatic rash" (Bottoms). As Bottoms writes in his article the young men who were employed as guards in the experiment intuited different ways to torture and harass those employed as prisoners. Bottoms writes:

> Although initially scheduled to last two weeks, Zimbardo's experiment was brought to a premature halt after just six days, because of concerns that some of the guards had begun reveling sadistically in their positions. Although physical violence was prohibited by the experiment's protocols, the guards had taken to devising even more elaborate rituals of staged humiliation and degradation for the prisoners.

Zimbardo and his associates write in their further analysis of the Stanford Prison Experiment that:

> Attempts to provide an explanation for the deplorable condition of our penal system and its dehumanizing effects upon prisoners and guards often focus upon what might be called the dispositional hypothesis, namely, "that the state of the social institution of prison is due to the 'nature' of the people who administrate it, or the 'nature' of the people who populate it, or both." (Haney)

I tend to disagree with this perception or analysis of the Stanford Prison Experiment and also all forms of prison environments and captivity for the reason that individuals who are a part of the prison, or society which holds men and women captive are of less importance than the grand overall, or macrocosmic consciousness which tends to pervade within and without society and its participants and which is rather transparent. The individuals enacting cruelty are subject to the oscillating, moving motivations and intuitions which reside within them and which may be called subconscious and visceral. Decisions made by those in a position of power tend to lose context as per those individuals' former conceptions and motivations and take on a life, or will of their own. Many times, victimization of one sort or another is the result as in the fascist movement in Europe in the mid-twentieth century and in the race riots in the 1960s. When looking at social action in a microcosmic level such as in Philip Zimbardo's Sanford Prison Experiment dispersion of stigmata are not as clear-cut and flawless as said dispersion is in a live, macrocosmic level. Bottoms writes, "The twenty-four subjects thus selected were then allocated, literally by the flip of a coin, to the role of guard or prisoner." This symmetric division of fate and the perfect separation of chance is not present in pedigree as per biologists' and anthropologists' claims on racial heredity. Symmetry and chance are not present in demographics either as is the case in the political theatre when regarding the surfacing of Bolshevism and the Nazi regime. Nor are symmetry and chance present in the judgement of individuals from a mental health professional standpoint. The arrival and perpetuation of these societal and political entities and their respective stigmata arrive and are perpetuated by role-playing psychologies and blind, or visceral obedience. A study which preceded Philip Zimbardo's Stanford Prison Experiment and which is just as famous is the Milgram's experiment. Bottoms writes in regards to the inspiration and forefather of the Stanford Prison Experiment, the Milgram's experiment that,

> Much of the fascination with Milgram's work stemmed from the strangely theatrical set- up of his experiment: volunteer participants were asked to act as 'teacher' in a (fake) learning scenario, and to administer ever-rising voltages of (fake) electric shock to a 'learner' in the next room—ostensibly to see if the shocks helped improve memory retention. Milgram's extraordinary ending was that fully 65 percent of his participants obediently went all the way to the lethal end of the shock scale, when pressured to do so by a white-coated scientist.

ANDERS M. SVENNING

This study which took place in July 1961 is evidence to the layman's submissiveness when in the presence of an individual in a position of power. The blatant disregard for one's own wellbeing is startling and scary when taking into account the masochistic derivation of knowledge, power, and even in some cases enlightenment by these individuals in positions of power. Joanna "Hannah" Arendt, a German-born Jewish American political theorist coined the phrase "the banality of evil" when regarding such dismissiveness in sociological settings of such violence, pain, and pococurante attitudes following the 1961 war crime trial of Adolf Eichmann. The article written by Bottoms reads: "'The prison system,' Zimbardo told his questioners, 'is guaranteed to generate severe enough pathological reactions in both guards and prisoners as to debase their humanity.'" It is misfortunate that prison systems are not only systems, or institutions bordered by cement walls and barbed wire fences and guard towers but also entities as common and accepted as the ivory tower, monetary policy, and the electoral system which too "generate severe enough pathological reactions" (Bottoms) but the pathological reactions take place not in guards and prisoners; the pathological reactions take place in the youth and the geriatric populace, the female, sex deviant, and even male populace, and of course the mental deviant and spiritual sensitive populace. Philip Zimbardo's *The Lucifer Effect* rehashes tantamount details regarding social psychology and the Sanford Prison Experiment with a few new realizations. Philip Zimbardo in *The Lucifer Effect* writes:

LIFE AFTER SCHIZOPHRENIA

[T]ypically, roles are tied to specific situations, jobs, and functions [and] can usually be set aside when one returns to his or her 'normal' other life. Yet some roles are insidious... they can become who we are most of the time. They are internalized even as we initially acknowledge them as artificial.

The internalization and recapitulation of the roles in specific situations i.e. jobs and their functions compels many times the professional and role-playing individual into embodying their roles on a more intimate, personal, and in some cases total level even when in nonprofessional or normal settings. This change, internalization, or recapitulation of identity, or role will be further discussed in the fifth and final essay in this book titled "Schizophrenia and the Spiritual Nature of the Human" and can be paraphrased into an aphorism: the loss of soul.

When dementia præcox was excised from the mental health catalogue of diagnoses by Paul Eugen Blueler, schizophrenia taking its place, the substitutive, or categorical symptoms which comprised and enabled the diagnosis of schizophrenia and which made the diagnosis to the mental health professional considerable quite remained. The value of these symptoms as we have established and which include but are not limited to so called hallucinations of the auditory and optical type and so called delusions such as heightened awareness of spirituality and religious intuition are differentiated, or held separate by the perceptions of their presence as good or bad as perceived by both the spiritual and religious advanced and the mental health professional. We have established this fact and there is no need to rehash the concept of values and morality, applicable means and practical means of these supposed symptoms for the remainder of this book. The acknowledgement of the intrinsic system of morality, value, and definition and the uses of language to depict the malignancy or goodness of said symptoms is a good place from which to peer into the fourth element of belief systems. The fourth element of belief systems reads: "Language, It is the logic of a belief system. Language of a belief system is composed of the logical rules which relate one substantive belief to another within the belief system [by means of an effective argument]" (Uso-Domenech and Nescolarde-Selva). In the case of schizophrenia, the effective argument that fortifies the theory's existence is the supposed fake, or baseless nature of the above symptoms which are in themselves means for validating the prescience of the diagnosis schizophrenia. Uso-Domenech and Nescolarde-Selva write in their article, "An argument is formed by the sum of two characteristics: (a) hypothesis: that is to say, so what is this physical and social reality? And (b) goal: we want this society to reach its 'perfection' (utopia)." Schizophrenia is absent on the physical level as established—it exists only in an epistemological and performative sense making it quite active in society—and the longing for perfection, or utopia is a self-righteous, idealistic goal which seems to be the case and present within the mental health professional as per their constant attempts at manipulating patients, or spiritual and religious advanced individuals and in effect society as a whole. The intricate machine that is society is comprised of many perspectives which scrutinize type after type and concept after concept. People identifying and capitulating schizophrenia will have differing perspectives on the subject like the viewing of a garden at different angles and may experience feelings quite close to *jamais vu* doing so, in most especial cases when belief systems are just starting to take hold in the individual and when a value system is in infancy. The fifth element of belief systems sets forth the concept of perspectives in a social setting within which many and differing types of people from different ethnicities and belief systems reside and interact. The fifth element of a belief system:

> Perspective, The perspective of a belief system or their cognitive map is the set of conceptual tools. Central in most perspectives is some statement of where the belief system and/or social group that carries it stands in relation to other things, specially nature, social events or other social groups. Are we equals? Enemies? Rulers? Friends? Perspective as description of the social environment is a description of the social group itself, and the place of each individual in it. The perspective may be stated as a myth. It explains not only who subjects are and how subjects came to be in cognitive terms, but also why subjects exist in terms of ideal values. Meaning and identification are provided along with cognitive orientation. (Uso-Domenech and Nescolarde-Selva)

Hierarchy, intrinsic motivation, and even mirthful emasculation of misfortunate and impoverished individuals seems to be a theme throughout the social universe from the

Roman Empire to present day religious radicalism. There is a cognitive orientation in these circumstances and there is no question the desire to establish dominance, retain superiority, and capitalize on social status exists in just as well every case in which there are two or more people present. While some individuals assume a passive role in this exchange and others assume a more aggressive role the seeming barbaric tendency remains in all organisms belonging to the Animalia kingdom, the Plantæ kingdom, and even in geology. It is a part of all existing beings to vary and perpetuate themselves for the good of their species and descendants. Like species of animals and types of plants theories, too, vary and perpetuate and transform as time elapses as is insinuated in the sixth element of belief systems:

> Prescriptions and Proscriptions, This includes action alternatives or policy recommendations as well as deontical norms for behavior. Historical examples of prescriptions are the Marx's *Communist Manifesto*, the Lenin's *What is To Be Done* or the Hitler's *Mein Kampf*. Deontical norms represent the cleanest connection between the abstract ideas and the concrete applied beliefs because they refer to behavior that is observable. They are the most responsive conditions in being directly carried by the social group through the mechanisms of social reward and punishment. (Uso-Domenech and Nescolarde-Selva)

LIFE AFTER SCHIZOPHRENIA

Bases of infant belief systems include the prognostications, analyzations, and even the squandering of a present norm from, for example, state politics to socio-economics to stereotypes. In the context of this book the prognostication and analyzation and squandering is applied to not a political, socio-economic, or stereotypical state but rather a state of mind. The above element of belief systems establishes the necessity for "the cleanest connection between the abstract ideas and the concrete applied beliefs" (Uso-Domenech and Nescolarde-Selva) in order to establish a considerable or substantial belief system. The above element of belief systems continues to suggest a responsive condition to a set group believing in a particular belief system, a responsive condition in other words meaning social reward and punishment. Regarding the schizophrenic populace social reward is nonexistent outside of the bolstering and motivational clap on the back signifying the triumph over schizophrenia, or schizophrenic symptoms. But, the individual who has been diagnosed with schizophrenia and also his or her family has been tainted on a societal level and marked vulnerable as far as genetics taking into account scientists' and mental health professionals' studies and belief systems. All of this removes the freewill of not only the individual experiencing the phenomenon known as schizophrenia but the freewill of the family from a macrocosmic and genetic level.

Prescriptions for affecting individuals or a group of people, as is the aim of the mental health professional, were at one point, as the sixth element of belief systems states, defined as political, economic, and societal doctrines written by intellectuals. The treating of mental ailments on an individualistic or societal basis is now delivered, or attempted to be delivered via synthetic chemicals, or medication. The term deonitic which is defined as relating to duty and obligation as ethical concepts and which is intended to perpetuate freewill and freedom for the people and society is counterintuitive in the context of schizophrenia and its treatment.

The seventh and final element of belief systems takes into account the ideological technologies, or symbols incorporated to symbolize a people. The schizophrenic populace, however, are not symbolized by a flag or talisman as are heritages, nations, and the queer population. The schizophrenic populace are bound together by means of an ethereal and universal understanding and are scattered throughout the world rather lost, autometronic, and of no consequence. Uso-Domenech and Nescolarde-Selva, defining the seventh element of belief systems, write:

> Ideological Technology, Every belief system contains associated beliefs concerning means to attain ideal values. Some such associated beliefs concern the subjective legitimacy or appropriateness of d-significances, while others concern only the effectiveness of various d-significances. For example, political activists and organizational strategy and tactics are properly called the technology of the belief system. Ideological Technology is composed of the associated beliefs and material tools providing means for the immediate or distant (Utopian) goals of a belief system. Ideological Technology is not

used to justify or validate other elements of a belief system, although the existence of ideological technologies may limit alternatives among substantive beliefs. Ideological Technology commands less commitment from believers than do the other elements. A change in Ideological Technology (strategy) may be responsible for changes in logical prior elements of a belief system. Ideological Technology, like belonging to the Structural Base [of a theory] and having a series of prescriptions concerning doing can influence the life conditions of believers, thus forcing an adaptation in the belief system itself.

The concept of freewill is spiritual and religious in its origin. The liberation not of corporeal bodies but of temporal, spiritual, and religious bodies is the aim of this book. The headless entity schizophrenia and the belief and blind faithfulness in its prescience makes this aim hard to accomplish. The most severe form of captivity is not that of corporeal, or material imprisonment nor is it the most horrible. Imprisonment of the mind is the most subversive and omnipresent type of captivity the human has ever experienced and it is in motion right now. For captivity to be present there must be at least two entities. One, the slaver; and two, the submitter. Luck plays a part when considering the skewing of these boundaries but luck also plays a part in the conscious shift of faith toward an entity who or which can organize a listless people. Uso-Domenech and Nescolarde-Selva close their article in stating:

Conflict between two groups, including war, may be defined as a battle between belief systems. Symbols emerge strongly in such conflicts: they may be revered objects like stones, writings, buildings, flags or badges; whatever they may be, they may symbolize the central core of belief systems. When people become symbols, the real person may become obscured behind the projected symbolic image or person. Organizations develop their own in-house culture and belief system, too, which leads them to act and behave in ways that might not seem entirely rational to an outsider.

Irrationality to an outsider as far as behavior and action is most the case when considering schizophrenia and the schizophrenic populace. Motivations come from somewhere and the behaviors and actions which are their derivatives are for the betterment of the individual. As written above, sometimes these motivations can be visceral. Sometimes they can be divine. But, they are always homeostatic in nature!

This is the conclusion of the theoretical part of this book. It is a necessity when taking into account the radical beliefs, thought forms, and actions believed, thought, and committed in conjunction with the diagnosis schizophrenia. It is a necessity when considering the root of the theory's existence and its subtle yet provocative role in spirituality and religion.

LIFE AFTER SCHIZOPHRENIA

Schizophrenia and the Social Behaviors of those
Misdiagnosed: Statistics, Observations, and Camaraderie

The theoretical portion of this book finished we will segue into
a couple of essays pertaining to anecdotal instances regarding
schizophrenia, the schizophrenic populace, and the mental
health industry. This essay while essential when attempting to
understand the life of a schizophrenic patient or those affected
by schizophrenia on a performative basis is brief; this essay
as opposed to the previous two essays is rather humorous. I
understand schizophrenia is not a comedic matter nor a matter
which should be taken with lightheartedness. Many have been
affected by schizophrenia and the hysteria perpetuating it and
many have been affected adverse to good and humanistic
intentions. That being said, what cannot be cleaned or purged
by conversation between two people or groups of people must
be enlivened by a dash of humor.

Years ago—I believe it was in the year 2013—in the state of
Florida, two friends with whom I have grown up from
adolescence into young adulthood and I went out for some
drinks at a local bar which has four or five billiards tables,
a ping pong table, and a bar centered in the establishment,
an establishment which not many frequent and which is
patronized by a tight knit group of people who know and are
aware of the very most inner and even darkest secrets of one
another. But, that is young adulthood at its finest and I dare say
the finest aspect of the sub-tropics as a whole.

Drinks having been ordered and consumed with methodical sureness, the conversation of schizophrenia surfaced for no other reason than the misfortunate association between the diagnosis and my two friends with whom I had gone out for drinks that evening; that is, two individuals who were diagnosed with schizophrenia and who were part of the same group of friends were in the same bar, drinking, and discussing their experiences with the phenomena. I listened attentive and spoke at times when something surfaced in my own inner dialogue and as the night went on and more people entered the bar, ordered drinks, and began utilizing the billiards tables and the ping pong table the conversation which was occurring between our three close friends became a conversation taking place in a large group of individuals, some of whom our three close friends did not know; and it came about that one of the new additions to the conversation had also been diagnosed with schizophrenia and had resumed functionality in public and in society without difficulty. Now, to somebody who is cynical and in the same establishment as three individuals diagnosed with schizophrenia, the awareness of the ill camaraderie may be jarring and perhaps even frightening. The conversation ended on the note of the hysterical pandemic of schizophrenia in the twenty-first century. I looked around and made a head count. There were thirty people in attendance in total at the bar that night.

This anecdote, I knew, I would have to include in the book the reader now holds in his or her hands as per the spike, or skyrocketed statistics in the diagnosis of schizophrenia. To put the incredulous idea in perspective a 2009 study beside a 2017 study on the prevalence of schizophrenia is quite called for. The 2009 study has been published in an article written by Messias, E., Chen, C., and Eaton, W. W. and is titled "Epidemiology of Schizophrenia: Review of Findings and Myths." Messias and associates write in regards to the 2009 statistics of schizophrenia diagnosis: "The range in annual incidence in schizophrenia is from 0.11/1000/year to 0.70/1000/year, and this range would not be much affected if several dozens of other studies, reviewed elsewhere, were included." While higher and vaster beside a study which, for instance, would have been taken in 1970, the 2009 study and statistic is not too mind shattering. That 1 in every 10,000 people to 7 in every 10,000 people have been diagnosed with schizophrenia is acceptable in terms of numbers and is not a hard number to swallow when taking into account verifiable claims, or instances of true psychotic symptoms such as threats to one's self and others for baseless reasons or inappropriate behavior in public or even in a familial setting.

The present statistics, however, when regarding the diagnosis schizophrenia are rather startling and have not only myself questioning the basis of such indiscriminate diagnoses but many a mental health professional, family member, and friend included. A 2017 study which has been published in *Psychiatry Research* and which has been published in an article titled "Daily life evidence of environment-incongruent emotion in schizophrenia" reads that, "At some time during their life about 1 in 100 people will suffer an episode of schizophrenia" (Sanchez). An increase of 1,000% has been noted and published in regards to the prevalence and diagnosis of schizophrenia from the mental health professional. This number is staggering and rather disturbing. It demarcates the value of the diagnosis but also the schizophrenic populace as a whole. True psychotic symptoms cannot be this much more prevalent over the course of only eight years. The rate of true psychotic individuals is the same as they were in the year 2009. The only difference between the year 2009 and the year 2017 insofar as the totality of schizophrenic ideology is the momentum is has built between those years; for the lack of a better term the bandwagon effect has taken place much like the television mini series craze and the nutrition craze. The evident presence of schizophrenia and its prescience among the mental health professional and those patients who accept such a hasty and even haphazard diagnosis in fact puts many at risk, social groups, the diagnosed, their families, and even the mental health professional and their families for many reasons and on many levels. The quickness of diagnosis and the striving for individualistic perfection, health, and functionality and the attempted apprehension of utopia is quite counter intuitive. In the same article which published the most recent statistic on the omnipresence of schizophrenia it is also written that, "Schizophrenia is a killer. Sufferers have a 1 in 10 chance of dying by their own hand within ten years of diagnosis" (Sanchez). I for one refuse to believe frequent, or commonplace euthanasia among the schizophrenic populace is due to true psychotic symptoms or depression. I for one believe the causal aspect of such prevalent euthanasia is the miasmic manifestation which has occurred in the lives of the misdiagnosed and which is a peripheral murderer of intelligent and even spiritual and religious advanced individuals as a commixing of medication side effects, internal notions of failure and vanity, and the constant and broadcasted message of ineptitude. That sufferers of the diagnosis schizophrenia have a 1 in 10 chance of euthanizing only solidifies my theory that a diagnosis, or misdiagnosis and euthanasia in these cases are two sides of the same coin. For these individuals who commit or even attempt to commit the act of euthanasia the diagnosis and the atrocious act are one in the same; you do not get one without the other; they go hand in hand. It is rather stark mad and frightening, the confidence with which mental health professionals in the present day dictate mental illness and the submissiveness of those who have received the diagnosis and who disagree with it, claiming higher realms of thought and functionality only to be chastised and lambasted in the sphere of professionalism, society, and even on familial bases, only to remove themselves from existence in totality by means of euthanasia.

Lencz and Malhotra have written an article which claims the genetic attraction, or magnetic attraction of protein compounds with genes that are predisposed to schizophrenia. The study published by Lencz and Malhotra take into account synthetic chemicals otherwise known as medication which affect schizophrenic susceptible genetic composition. This of course is mere speculation taking into account the "correlation does not mean causation" theory which goes back well over one hundred years in psychological theory and which contemporary scientists seem to dismiss. The study published by Lencz and Malhotra set out to find the peculiar connection between genetic targets otherwise known as established targets to which antipsychotic drugs attach, making the genetic target in question a liable case for schizophrenic predisposition. The concept seems rather idealistic. The study in any case published their findings in an article titled "Targeting the Schizophrenia Genome: A Fast Track Strategy from GWAS to Clinic" written by T. Lencz and A.K. Malhotra.:

> Of the 1,030 druggable genes, 555 unique genes were identified that serve as targets of approved pharmaceuticals, which they refer to as "established targets." An additional 475 genes were targeted by compounds in registered clinical trials, referred to as "novel targets." The full list of 1,030 drug targets represents 5.06% of all genes (based on the GENCODE21 version 19, July 2013 freeze, which estimates the total number of protein-coding genes in the human genome at 20,345) [predisposed to schizophrenia].

The cause of such non-placated diagnoses is not confined to mere genetics. Further studies which will be expounded upon below and which regard environmental effects on the human mind will be depicted. Scientists of late are attempting to create a microcosm of chemicals and molecular symbiosis in relation to the mentalities of men and women. This approach to the intimacies of man is a misfortunate approach and rather disregards the elements of humanism which the study of psychology was founded upon with such popularity. Furthermore, the Lencz and Malhotra article states that, "Gene products were only considered to be true drug targets if direct binding had been demonstrated; indirect effects of up- or down-regulation were not included." There is some news, or aspectual factors which these scientists refuse to acknowledge. That is the genetic makeup of individuals are not the same as they were from birth or childhood. The fact that these scientists are looking for genetic "predisposition" in individuals is voided by causation including but not limited to substance use, viruses, and even environmental factors. This fact is cause enough to send the neuroscientific notion of predisposed mental health issues into the refuse realm of thought. Genetic makeup is not set in stone. It is not a stone slab into which a secretive or mystical code is chiseled. The genetic code of an individual changes over time and is affected by elements such as drug usage (street or prescribed drugs), diseases chronic and ephemeral such as AIDS (Auto Immune Deficiency Syndrome) and Zika virus, varicella otherwise known as chicken pocks, and even environmental factors such as climate, that is humidity, temperature, and water systems in a given location. The human genome is that sensitive and susceptible to change. Rather than looking at a biophysical factor of schizophrenic predispositions, environmental, socio-economical, intrinsic and even familial senses of self, self-deprecation, and notions of vanity and inferiority come into play when regarding so called psychotic symptoms, as stated in Brown and Lau's article titled "Chapter 2: A Review of the Epidemiology of Schizophrenia. *Handbook Of Behavioral Neuroscience, 23* (Modeling the Psychopathological Dimensions of Schizophrenia)." Brown and Lau go on to state that in some individuals a phenomenon known as culture shock, or acculturation can induce an unexpected set of circumstances, or mentalities which are rather unorthodox and can be called by the common mental health professional as psychotic. They state that in some individuals, children in particular, the change in setting is traumatic enough to induce unexplainable sensations and perceptions:

> First- and second-generation migrants have a higher risk of schizophrenia. This idea was originally presented in a paper by Odegaard (1932), who found that Norwegian immigrants in the United States were more likely to be admitted to the hospital for schizophrenia compared with Norwegians born in the United States or those who still lived in Norway. Cantor-Graae and Selten (2005) followed up on this idea, finding a higher incidence of schizophrenia among subjects in the United Kingdom who originally had an African Caribbean background; individuals in the Netherlands with a Surinamese, Dutch Antillean, or Moroccan background; and subjects of various ethnic backgrounds in Denmark. In addition, subjects who immigrated from a developing country were more likely to develop schizophrenia than those from a developed country.

This aspect of the human psychology is called acculturation and is very prevalent in children who move from extreme climate or society to the opposite extreme climate, from metropolitan setting to rural setting or from a setting of racial likeness to a setting of racial difference. It is not an innate bigotry that makes these children susceptible to influences regarding practical and actual likenesses insofar as their living environment. It is a simple sensational effect much like the shock one feels when jumping into a pool of cold water and sustaining the physical consequences as if an undying member of the polar bear club. Uncertainty, anxiety, and acculturation take place without a shadow of a doubt in drastic changes in setting, climate, and even familial and community changes; individuals subject to this inexplicable change are affected by anxiety in an otherwise alien culture or environment. This semblance however takes place not only in children but in individuals who are experiencing high pressure circumstances in a socioeconomic level and who are in fact associated with a lower social selectiveness. Brown and Lau write in their article:

> They found an especially high risk of schizophrenia for migrants in Europe from countries with high black populations; this finding was replicated in further studies. Dealberto (2010) suggested that vitamin D deficiency in dark-skinned individuals might be responsible for this higher rate of schizophrenia. Cantor-Graae and Selten (2005) proposed an alternative explanation for their findings, namely the experience of social defeat, which they define as a subordinate position in society or an outsider status. The authors suggested that the chronic experience of social defeat through high competition in jobs, housing, and other aspects of life leads to increased sensitivity in the mesolimbic dopamine system. In support of this

> theory, the authors observed that immigrant groups who suffer from a low socioeconomic status in a highly competitive atmosphere have the highest risks for schizophrenia, although this association may be due to social selection rather than social causation.

As stated in the quote above the effects of societal and cultural changes which can be drastic and which can be detrimental to some young or unprepared individuals are not limited to socioeconomic and familial bases but also on a neurological basis which takes into account the volatility of vulnerable and one could say whimsical individuals, or children. The individual or child in question detects the change in their environment, whether it be an economical, social, or climactic change and their psychologies, disposition, and even their genetic makeup change in accordance. In some misfortunate circumstances a negative pattern of thought takes place, otherwise known as mood congruent perception or memories. An individual experiencing this unfortunate bout of internal thoughts descends into unhappy and even visceral aspects of thoughts which excite symptoms otherwise known as psychotic symptoms. The descending of a healthy state of mind into the unhealthy, or even visceral state of mind which can be described as the downward spiraling mentality and which is correlated with so called psychotic or supernatural experiences or exchanges is subject and symbiotic with predominance to a physics theory mathematical in nature discovered by an individual named Stanislaw Ulam in 1963, otherwise known as the Ulam's spiral, or prime spiral. There is that much irony in the human consciousness; one could even call it perfection.

The scientist named Stanislaw Ulam who discovered the connection between the conscious and the subconscious mind was born in 1909 and made his reputation with his unexpected series of discoveries in set theory, topology, measure theory and functional analysis. The totality of Ulam's studies which are infused with the psychologic and mathematical composition of the human psychology focus on three paradigms: coherent structures and solitons, deterministic chaos and fractals, and complex configuration and patterns otherwise known as nonlinear science—all of which Ulam with simplicity called science. To put these notions in context I will go through their definitions with brevity. Coherent structures are the common logistical structures which flow and which are coherent as per their outcomes like algebraic equations or any basic mathematical equation for that matter. Solitons are three dimensional structures which are derivatives of basic mathematical equations and which retain their shapes through thick and thin like a cylinder or a box. They are unlike vortices, shock waves, surface waves, bubbles, flame fronts which are ephemeral in nature and which are in semblance with metaphysical human thought forms. Deterministic systems have a property that their state in time t is determined and unique to their initial state like the hours of the day or habitual tendencies like haircut appointments or the day in and day out consumption of coffee. Deterministic chaos is the irregular, unpredictable anomaly which occurs in deterministic systems like the second law of thermodynamics, in short defined as "Cosmos to Chaos," and which are peculiar insofar as their unpredictability like supposed psychotic symptoms and faulty machinery. Fractals are curves or geometric figures, each part of which has the same statistical character as the whole. This insinuates a growing, or lessening of size but to an exponential or rescinding effect which in nature can be found in the exponential broadening of seashells, the crystalized manifestation of snowflakes, the seeming unforeseeable directionality of lightening, and cognizant crystal formations and which belong to the deterministic chaos grouping of phenomena. Complex configurations are understood as collections of complex points, lines, planes, et cetera. In complex configurations the x-coordinate plane, the y-coordinate plane, and the z-coordinate (depth) plane are conjoined at many peculiar points and are the junctions of multiple lines, lines of multiple planes, and so on. A pattern thus is a repeating design. The abstractness into which Ulam has gone in the early twentieth century is not removed, not in the least, from human conscious-subconscious cognizance. In fact, the seeming coherent structures, or mathematical significances in actuality, the solutions, or three-dimensional constructions in the eyes, the deterministic systems such as the hours of the day and habitualness therein, the deterministic chaos and fractals which procure themselves in psychological ether and which are reflective of their material counterparts such as the snowflake or crystal formation, the complex configurations, or multi-dimensional contrivances of deterministic chaos and fractal systems and patterns are all quite imbued with the communication taking place between the conscious and subconscious minds. All these aspects are a part of and interwoven with Ulam's most famous conception, the Ulam's spiral, or the prime spiral. Ulam's spiral is constructed in its simple manner by writing the positive integers in a square spiral and marking the prime numbers in sequence. Both Stanislaw Ulam and an associate Dr. Gardner noted that "the existence of such prominent, intersecting lines is not unexpected, as lines in the Ulam's spiral, or prime spiral correspond to quadratic polynomials[1], and certain such polynomials, such as Euler's prime-generating polynomial[2] $x^2 - x + 41$, are believed to produce a high density of prime numbers" (Lax). These prime numerical recurrences are in semblance with the time-space continuum which is a derivative of consciousness in entirety and its analogousness and which is in semblance with conscious mind and subconscious mind communication. The final essay in this book will expound on such introspective communication. But, insofar as Ulam's and Gardner's intention when contriving the spiral it was meant to exhibit supposed incognizant or elemental modes of existence and numerical units of value. The spiral and its seeming role in contemporary existence was rather accidental or unexpected in its discovery as well:

> According to Gardner, Ulam discovered the spiral in 1963 while doodling during the presentation of "a long and very boring paper" at a scientific meeting. These hand calculations amounted to "a few

---

1. https://en.wikipedia.org/wiki/Quadratic_function

2. https://en.wikipedia.org/wiki/
   Formula_for_primes%2523Prime_formulas_and_polynomial_functions

hundred points." Shortly afterwards, Ulam, with collaborators Myron Stein and Mark Wells, used MANIAC II at Los Alamos Scientific Laboratory to extend the calculation to about 100,000 points. The group also computed the density of primes among numbers up to 10,000,000 along some of the prime-rich lines as well as along some of the prime-poor lines. Images of the spiral up to 65,000 points were displayed on "a scope attached to the machine" and then photographed. The Ulam spiral was described in Martin Gardner's March 1964 *Mathematical Games* column in *Scientific American* and featured on the front cover of that issue. Some of the photographs of Stein, Ulam, and Wells were reproduced in the column.

The spiral, taking into account its horizontal, vertical, and diagonal components on an integral level creates of the line segments and the formulæ used to exponentiate them an interwoven manifestation which is a non-linear anomaly in nature composed of linear lines, a dimensional continuum of sorts, and which is essential to Albert Einstein's theory of relativity regarding light and a moving steam engine. All theories and conceptions regarding physics are essential units in the formulaic conscious-subconscious relation which is a temporal, that is time-space oriented, relation in nature and which will be expounded upon in the final essay within this book.

LIFE AFTER SCHIZOPHRENIA

This dichotomous aspect of the human mind in its physical nature is not so different from its mathematical or even environmental nature. The communication taking place between the conscious mind and the subconscious mind is delicate and can be thrown off balance by effects which seem harmless and which Brown and Lau state are detrimental in nature to some peculiar individuals. They write: "Studies have consistently shown that being raised in an urban setting leads to a higher risk of developing schizophrenia and that this risk is related to the level of urbanicity in a dose–response relationship." This statement takes into account the effectuality of urbanicity in those misdiagnosed with schizophrenia. But, this fact as written in Brown and Lau's article is rather incomplete and tells only of one half of the idea. The notion depicting urban setting and schizophrenia correlations with greater prevalence neglects the populace of individuals who are affected in adverse ways by seeming deprived or ruralist settings of homes. For some individuals the high-paced, or up-tempo way of urban life can affect the mind to a detrimental, or deprecating degree. But, to others the urban way of life is a necessity, taking into account the deprived, ruralist, and rather unorganized way of life prevalent in so called uncivilized, or rustic ways of life. No two individuals are the same. And if two individuals are the same they may as well be differentiated for the sake of humanism. The study regarding metropolitanism and schizophrenia goes on to state: "Finally, a recent study by Sariaslan et al. (2015) found that population density as measured when the subject was 15 years of age was a predictor of later schizophrenia." If urbanicity can affect one in detrimental ways then ruralism can affect the other in the same way. This is the dichotomous, or two fold way in which we all live. Learn to like it. Outside of neurochemical indicators or causes of so called psychotic symptoms, the writers of "Chapter 2: A Review of the Epidemiology of Schizophrenia. *Handbook Of Behavioral Neuroscience, 23* (Modeling the Psychopathological Dimensions of Schizophrenia)," that is Brown and Lau, state potential explanations for so called schizophrenic symptoms are, "individual or family characteristics, selective migration, a greater risk of being exposed to infections or pollutants, an insufficient diet, or a poor social environment." In addition, the authors point to social fragmentation and deprivation as a possible explanation. But, this deprivation is not limited to malnutrition or social deprivation. Intellectual and spiritual deprivation play a part in the insufficient development of an individual and in most especial cases in the individual at or around fifteen years of age. Also, deprivation on a traditional or subconscious and genealogical level can play a part in the malnourishment of not only an individual's body but also an individual's mind. Climate, from temperate to tropic or from tropic to temperate can affect an individual's mindset, and so can the sanitariness of the food and water at hand in a given location. Brown and Lau go on to state in regards to this environmental catalyst of supposed psychosis:

> It is unlikely that the environmental exposures reviewed here act alone to cause psychopathology[3]. Rather, many investigators have proposed integrative, or diathesis–stress models, that

---

3. http://www.sciencedirect.com/topics/page/Psychopathology

incorporate genetic influences, including interactions between genetic mutations and environmental factors. According to this model, by interacting with genetic influences, these environmental factors impact development of the brain during critical periods and trigger the onset of psychotic syndromes such as schizophrenia[4]. Various environmental influences act on sensitive subgroups of the population with a genetic predisposition to such environmental effects.

It is true that no one aspect can be responsible for the entire mental shift of an individual. The human being is an organism and not a machine. The human being acts as a singular entity. The human being is not made of interchangeable parts like an industrious machine, complacent and dismissive of internal and external changes.

Potential explanations include individual or family characteristics, selective migration, a greater risk of being exposed to infections or pollutants, an insufficient diet, or a poor social environment. In addition, Brown and Lau point to social fragmentation and deprivation as a possible explanation. As aforementioned, the genetic makeup of a given individual is not composed of and affected by infinitesimal and microscopic organisms; not always. Sometimes, the most influential and substantial changes in our genetic makeup, or physiognomy are caused by viruses, sicknesses, consumption of synthetic or organic substances, et cetera, and even air quality, humidity, and the quality of water. All these potential causes of so called

4. http://www.sciencedirect.com/topics/page/Schizophrenia

schizophrenic, or supernatural or metaphysical development in the spiritual and religious advanced individual are peculiar to the individual, rare but more prevalent than one would expect. Brown and Lau go on to state that the causation of so called schizophrenic symptoms, or elevated perceptions as per drastic changes in environment and in effect physiognomy are, in a neuro-molecular level, related to but not confined to proteins in the human brain:

> One example of a gene–environment interaction is provided by a potential relationship between the genes that encode the major histocompatibility complex[5] class I proteins, which have been associated with schizophrenia in genome-wide association studies[6]... These proteins are necessary for proper functioning of not only T lymphocytes[7], but also synaptic function. It has been suggested that individuals with these mutations are more sensitive to the effects of a prenatal infection or other environmental events that activate the immune system[8].

The unexpected effects of such environmental, societal, and in effect neurological changes are in semblance with a subconscious rejection of habitat. But, while this subconscious rejection is taking place and while supposed unexplainable,

5. http://www.sciencedirect.com/topics/page/Major_histocompatibility_complex

6. http://www.sciencedirect.com/topics/page/Genome-wide_association_study

7. http://www.sciencedirect.com/topics/page/T_cells

8. http://www.sciencedirect.com/topics/page/Immune_system

metaphysical sensations in the spiritual and religious advanced individual are taking place one can also state that the mystery of the human mind is also at work. In children fifteen years of age or even in individuals reaching into their mid-twenties gestalt psychology, that is the implementation of environmental, societal, and intellectual aspects, in other words the completion of the deprived locale as per supernatural and in effect spiritual and even religious means, takes place. These sometimes whimsical but sometimes quite demanding puzzle pieces are necessary to the spiritual and religious advanced individual in question, but circumstances differ from case to case. In the context of this book, however, those who are in fact experiencing metaphysical and supernatural phenomena and those who are replacing aspects of their former surroundings with higher sensation-perception faculties in their latter surroundings are in fact experiencing a transformative, or transcendental sequence of events. These trying circumstances, however, are not always hand in hand with flawless transformations. Depression, isolation, and even self-inflicted harm can be results of these otherworld, fantastical phenomena.

In such cases, mental health professionals and scientists alike have the gall to claim so called schizophrenic symptoms, psychotic trains of thought, and self-inflicted harm are rooted in the genetic compositions of the man or woman enacting these thoughts or actions.

Logic tells the reader that those who commit the deed of isolation and even euthanasia have been affected by negative, or morbid thoughts. There is no question of that and it would be foolish to dismiss the patients' apathy. The article written by A. Sanchez and associates conveys the prevalence of negative, or morbid thoughts and apathy in the schizophrenic populace. The abstract of the study reads:

> The current study used EMA, a methodology developed to measure experiences in-the moment, to investigate environment-incongruent negative emotion in the daily lives of people with and without schizophrenia. Research assistants called participants four times a day for a week, and asked them about their current emotional state (including several positive and negative emotions), their current activities, and how much they were enjoying these activities.

The study must be considered with its relativity to society as a macrocosm. Keeping this in mind the reader can make deductions pertaining to the schizophrenic populace with wariness. The article continues: "Our findings are in line with several studies that have shown intact hedonic experience in schizophrenia, equivalent enjoyment of life activities in people with and without schizophrenia, but higher negative emotion in schizophrenia" (Sanchez). The higher negative emotions can and in all probability were related to the schizophrenic perception in society as a whole; but the entirety of the schizophrenic ideology lies, however, on the shoulders of the schizophrenic populace and the subjects taking part in a study as a sovereign entity which is titular as far as schizophrenia research is concerned and which is quite pressurized. The schizophrenic subjects in the study mentioned above are active individuals in the schizophrenic hysteria, have accepted their diagnosis and its inherent apathy, and unbeknownst to them gave the answers and responses which were expected by the study's proctors. This last notion cannot be dismissed and is known in the psychological field of study as sublimation which is defined as a mature type of defense mechanism where impulses and idealization not accepted by society are transformed by usage of the subconscious into actions or behaviors common and accepted by society. The participation in the study by the individuals is not unfortunate in its entirety as per the negative thinkers' participation in a group setting. Many times, once the diagnosis of schizophrenia has been donned on an individual, social life tends to take a minimal or less active role. This is not because of intolerance for the schizophrenic populace from the friends' or families' perspective, not always, but more so a closing up of or a sense of finality regarding or the cutting off from a former life as a result of the jarring diagnosis. Lipskaya-Velikovsky and associates define participation in occupation as follows:

Participation in occupation is a universal phenomenon, experienced by all people, regardless of their skills or talents, and it encompasses all human pursuits (mental, physical, social, and spiritual; restful, reflective, and active; obligatory and self-chosen; paid and unpaid). The importance of participation for survival, health, and well-being is so paramount that it is a basic human right.

It is in fact true and quite the case that participation in occupation is a basic human right as Lipskaya-Velikovsky and associates have called it. If participation in occupation were not a right the human being would be hermetic and rather divine, demonic, or both. The Lipskaya-Velikovsky article continues in relating participation in occupation with schizophrenia: "Schizophrenia affects participation through several mechanisms, such as cognitive, affective, and physical impairments, as well as through environmental restrictive factors." This fact has been established in this essay and even in the previous two essays. The cognitive, affective, and psychical impairments relate to ideological discrepancies, interpersonal exchanges, and confinement in the corporeal, spatial, and performative spheres of existence, and just as well any sphere of existence established in the first essay titled "Schizophrenia: Real or Imagined" which defines the epistemological, corporeal, temporal, performative, and spatial spheres of existence. Hospitalizations as per mental deviation can and will impair participation in occupation insofar as physical captivity (corporeal/spatial effects) , damaged or tainted reputations, or histories (temporal/epistemological effects), and trauma on the mental and physical level as a result of institutionalization (performative effects). These causations of impairments are quite dismissed by mental health professionals and people well-versed in mental illness. More common is the acknowledgement of impairments caused by psychotropic medications. Lipskaya-Velikovsky and associates close their article by stating that:

LIFE AFTER SCHIZOPHRENIA

The affective symptoms of schizophrenia include social withdrawal, apathy, hostility, and a lack of volition and motivation, which lead frequently to restriction in participation. Moreover, medication for schizophrenia symptoms sometimes leads to side effects, such as movement disorders (extra-pyramidal syndrome), that may limit participation.

I am implored to consider the chronological location of the affective symptoms of schizophrenia as Lipskaya-Velikovsky state are "social withdrawal, apathy, hostility, and a lack of volition and motivation" as the causation of a misdiagnosis or as the effect of a misdiagnosis. It is a notion worth exploring by mental health professionals and all else who believe more so in disorder rather than order. That three individuals diagnosed with schizophrenia were in attendance the night of the conversation which inspired this essay is evidence enough that treatment, medication and psychotherapy, are best when implemented in conjunction with a request by the diagnosed individual, making medication and psychotherapy voluntary. Two of the three individuals who were diagnosed with schizophrenia and who were in attendance that night have ceased accepting treatment, medication and psychotherapy, and maintain high functionality. The acceptance of psychotherapy which is a humanistic approach to treatment is not as misfortunate a choice as the acceptance of medication, a schizophrenic component which is created and perpetuated by an organized and criminalistic people and which is the subject of the next essay in this book.

Schizophrenia: The Green, the Guilty, and the Bamboozled

———

THE MEDICATION DISPENSED in the name of health as per Western standards of healing are rather similar to back alleys, in a figurative sense, through which one can slip and escape the realm of responsibility and rationale. Now, let me explain. The pills and the intramuscular medications prescribed to schizophrenic patients are peripheral, or by products of the actual motivation which propels the pharmaceutical industry to create them and the mental health professional to prescribe them. In one word, the motivation is called currency. In two words, the motivation is called heretical zealotry. In three words, the motivation is called ball and chain. Regardless of what one calls it—all of the terms which can be coined are rather inconsequential and nondescript—the industry, the money, the criminalistic individuals who operate within it and perpetuate it, and of course the misfortunate individuals who fall right into the booby trap are present, omnipresent even, and create a tempest of a confusing and rather porous fabric to which all are subject.

It is rather baffling and even comedic the way the industry which creates medicines for illnesses from cancer to the common cold, from schizophrenia to auto immune deficiency syndrome finds ways to manipulate not only its subjects who are not of a class substantial enough to make a tide turning change in medical ideology but also the mental health professional itself, corporations, and, yes, even the government. Whether the heads of the industry are taking the approach toward organized crime as an aircraft approaches enemy territory, that is at high altitude and invisible, or assuming a surefire and blatant presence in the face of the public and just as well any entity under their influence is not an issue. It is not an issue for the sole reason that over the recent ten years the industry's and its heads' foolery has been identified and people are beginning to publish works on the racketeering, in motion pictures and in the written word alike, and some are even taking to boycotting medication of any kind in entirety. Rather than taking this miasmic construction in one go and looking at it from a universal level, that is taking into account all forms of illness and medication, we shall continue our levelheaded scrutiny from the point of view of schizophrenia.

Vardi writes in an article titled "Another Drug Company That Raises Prices Like Crazy" a little bit about the space shuttle which is the price of psychotropic medication. It reads:

> Starting in April, a little-known generic drug company in Philadelphia suddenly raised the price of Fluphenazine, a medication used to treat symptoms of certain types of schizophrenia, by 1,650% over a three-month period. The evidence: Prescription tracking firm IMS Health discloses the number of times a medicine is prescribed and themedicine's gross sales. IMS tracked 32,072 prescriptions of Fluphenazine in the first three months of 2016, generating $358,000 and yielding a net price of $11.17. Between April and June, there

were 37,320 prescriptions at a net price of $195.53, generating $7.3million in sales over the three-month period.

The net price of a prescription of psychotropic medication coming out to a total of $195.53 is not that bad next to a psychotropic drug like Latuda which comes out to nearing $3,000 for a one month's supply. Fluphenazine is a generic drug which is sold for a lower price to individuals who are without upper end insurance policies and which seems to work well for the populace who takes the drug. In that regard, the makers of Fluphenazine are doing good deeds for lower income families which have within them individuals diagnosed with seeming psychotic symptoms. The voluntary ingestion of medication for these individuals could however be interchanged with humanistic pursuits in a psychotherapist's office and would as an effect be better off in their physiologies, mentalities, and in some cases their spiritualties. Ethics, however, is not the theme of this essay.

Psychotropic medication is an essential component in the pharmaceutical industry and is as per the worldwide hysteria over mental illness and schizophrenia expanding in production and revenue; it is only a partial piece of the gross profit in the whole of the global pharmaceutical industry. Vardi writes in the article aforementioned a note regarding the total revenue of the global pharmaceutical industry over the past fifteen years. The growth in revenue is extreme and disconcerting: "In 2001, worldwide revenue was around 390.2 billion U.S. dollars. Ten years later, this figure stood at some 963 billion U.S. dollars. In 2014, global pharmaceutical revenues for the first time increased to over one trillion U.S. dollars." This growth in total revenue has me, and many individuals around the world, questioning the validity of medication dispersal, creation, and research. The total revenue has tripled over the past fifteen years as the above numbers state and mental illness and sickness, violent incidents and epidemics are more prevalent than ever. The notion that cures have been discovered and covered up, the chemical formations burned in fire with all literalness is quite clear in mind and I would rather not expound on the notion of blood money in this essay or in this book in entirety. But, I have mentioned it and will leave the gravity of monetary capitalization of death, disease, violence, and madness to take its course and be brief and weightless in hopes the covered will be uncovered and the flames of conspiracy be extinguished.

If one were to constrict the eye, or pupil of a skeptic of the pharmaceutical industry and medication the eye would pick up in regards to the psychotropic branch of these corporations a number just around 80 billion when gaging the total revenue made from psychotropic medication. The numbers are too high. The prices asked by these corporations, the number of people prescribed to these medications, and the money expended to create these medications do not add up. Prices are high, demand is in abundance as is supply. This is simple economics. When a demand and a supply are high prices tend to be low as is the case in the fruit we all know and love: bananas. The inconsistent trend of high demand, high supply, and high prices is known as price gouging which is illegal is some states and is supposed to be mandated on a state government level. That price gouging is committed on a nationwide and worldwide level opens passages of escape and many criminalistic possibilities. Law enforcement comes up short once more. Legislation and the executive cabinets do not attempt to reign in this bucking and kicking equus caballus of an organization.

In the state of Mississippi following the disaster hurricane Katrina an individual named John Shepperson made news headlines and the story grew into a nationwide sensation. Following the announcement made by Mississippi Attorney General Jim Hood who declared the state law enforcement officers would crack down on price gouging many arrests were made and one peculiar individual was arrested, our gouger named John Shepperson who lived in Kentucky at the time of hurricane Katrina and decided to collect electric generators and sell them to families affected by the disaster. John Shepperson bought nineteen electric generators, loaded them up in a U-haul, and drove 600 miles down to an area in Mississippi that had lost power in the wake of the disaster. As is the case with psychotropic medication demand was high for electric generators and supply was at hand. It is true that John Shepperson intended to sell the electric generators for twice the price at which he bought them, an intention which was enacted and which was the cause of his eventual arrest. Yet, people still bought the electric generators. In the middle of a sale, Mississippi law enforcement crashed the event and took John Shepperson off to jail where he spent in close quarters with genuine criminals the next four days. His generators are said to be still in police custody. This is mere anecdotal evidence of what law enforcement is capable of when taking into account a supposed delineation in morality and economics. It tends to be the case when regarding the behemoth that is the pharmaceutical industry that when morality and economics are in question the ability to intervene is rather disregarded. In fact, a governmental exchange with the corporations which compose the pharmaceutical industry would be as per the megalomaniacal power in global infatuation and dependence on medicine vain and dangerous on levels not seen by the public and on levels which if perceived can be called undertones of a corporate regime-controlled globe.

Much has changed since the dawn of the psychotropic drug. Drugs today are said to have less intense side effects and can in many cases be used for effects which the mental health professional calls off label usage. The original psychotropic drugs, such as Haldol and Thorazine, were too intense when regarding side effects to be used for any other purpose than the treatment of psychotic symptoms and were prescribed to nobody else but the supposed psychotic. Togar and associates write on the side effects of antipsychotic medication in their article titled "The Genotoxic Potentials of some Atypical Antipsychotic Drugs on Human Lymphocytes":

> As the uses of antipsychotic medications increase, the number of overdoses continues to grow. And atypical antipsychotic treatment has been associated with serious adverse events. Many classes of psychiatric drugs including typical and atypical antipsychotics have been reported as possible causes

of haematological toxicity. Body weight gain and sexual/reproductive dysfunction are well-known serious consequences of atypical antipsychotics treatment. The overdoses of several atypical antipsychotics were also associated with testicular alterations, hepatotoxicity, cardiotoxicity, fatal acute intoxication and neuroleptic malignant syndrome.

All this jargon may well be over some individuals' heads. For all intents and purposes these drugs affect the reproductive system on hormonal levels to levels more shall we say psychological as per unfortunate realizations that one is after all this time and after all these chemicals sterile. This quote and its subsequent thought could just as well been included in the previous essay titled "Schizophrenia and the Social Behaviors of those Misdiagnosed: Statistics, Observations, and Camaraderie" which brings into question a misdiagnosed schizophrenic patients' social and familial life and exchanges. The twenty-first century antipsychotic and its side effects are no better than first generation antipsychotics in this regard. The ability to function when taking improved antipsychotic medication and not descending into catatonia as an effect of the administration of antipsychotic medicine is the only improvement that has been made since the turn of the century. All else regarding hormonal fluctuations, organ dysfunction and in effect the organs' inability to operate, and adverse affected hemoglobin as the only mere side effects are on the pharmaceutical industry's part selling points for their products which the FDA and mental health professionals across the globe believe and accept quite doubtless. Effects from antipsychotic medications such as olanzapine, or Zyprexa a drug which will be discussed at length below and other antipsychotic medications, as stated by Togar and associates, also had intense side effects but the side effects of olanzapine, or Zyprexa and a few other drugs were side effects of a different kind. Togar and associates write: "The long-term carcinogenesis assays performed on rats and mice exhibited positive results for OLZ (liver and mammary tumours), RPD (pituitary, pancreas and mammary tumours) and QTP (thyroid adenomas and mammary gland adenocarcinomas)." OLZ which is the abbreviation for olanzapine, or Zyprexa, RPD which is the abbreviation for risperidone, and QTP which is the abbreviation for quetiapine are all detrimental to the living organism, or living flesh but these three drugs are not the only antipsychotic medications that have tested positive for carcinogenic tendencies. There are many more antipsychotics on the market which have been undiscovered by the populace to be carcinogenic and which like olanzapine, or Zyprexa, risperidone, and quetiapine have been approved by the FDA. Be not fooled, however, that these invisible drugs' virulence has not been discovered by the pharmaceutical companies. The most disturbing aspect of all is that the drug manufactures being brought to trial such as the olanzapine, or Zyprexa manufacturers claim that these antipsychotic medicines are improved, progressive, and superior than the first-generation drugs in that they withhold from the worst mental side effects such as catatonia, erratic eye movement, and tachycardia. In fact, the side effects of these so called improved, progressive, and superior antipsychotic drugs affect not the mind but the vital and vulnerable organs. And the improved drugs on the market have now in the twenty-first century a wide range of consumers.

Today many drugs catalogued as psychotropics, or antipsychotics are used for their effects on states such as depression, anxiety, mania, and many other mental states. The drugs which are used predominant and universal in the twenty-first century for all mental deviated states and which are said to be superior to their predecessors are called second generation antipsychotics, or SGAs. Mossman writes in his article titled "Promoting, Prescribing, and Pushing Pills: Understanding the Lessons of Antipsychotic Drug Litigation" regarding the off-label usage of second generation antipsychotics, or SGAs: "By the early years of the twenty-first century, use of SGAs had expanded rapidly and extended well beyond treating schizophrenia and closely related psychotic disorders." This is considered by some a stroke of good luck, hard work paid off, or an advancement in mental health sciences. The hasty prescribed SGA is in fact rather unfortunate as the mental health world and the globe at large learned as a result of the 2007 lawsuits which involved the SGA olanzapine, or Zyprexa and which will be covered in depth in the succeeding paragraphs in this essay. The prescribing of not only olanzapine but just as well dozens of other SGAs had become like the diagnosis of schizophrenia utter hysteria; and while the prescribing of SGAs for off-label usages is in fact legal it likewise is not a usage which the FDA had approved on the SGAs' acceptance, or admittance into mental health offices and into circulation as is stated in the Mossman article:

> The rapid rise in expenditures for SGAs was due, in part, to physicians' prescribing more than one of these drugs at a time and to prescribing them "off-label." Off-label use—that is, prescribing a medication or using a medical device outside the scope of its FDA- approved labeling—is, in general, a perfectly legal practice [and] is very common and well accepted throughout medicine.

The off-label uses of SGAs are off-label for a reason. The SGAs are not meant to be prescribed for reasons outside of those delineated. It seems the mental health professional considers the psychotropic drug and more so the SGA as a miraculous drug, or force that can heal any mental issue. This is not the case and while it is unfortunate that drugs do not perform what they were intended to perform without harmful, or intense side effects the more severe problem does not lie in the faulty molecular composition of the drugs but in the mental health professional and the chemists and even the FDA members who prescribe, conjure, and approve such drugs with haste and zeal. In the lawsuits pertaining to olanzapine the patients, or victims had gotten compensated and quite compensated for the erroneous practices of all three at fault, the mental health professional, the chemists, and the FDA members who approved of the psychotropic drug olanzapine. All patients, or victims who have been affected by harmful, or intense side effects should be so fortunate to fall into the good and monetary bosom of the pharmaceutical industry. But, that is not the case and all are affected by the adverse experiences following the ingestion of psychotropics and their side effects when used for off-label uses and FDA-approved uses. Those patients who had been prescribed olanzapine found themselves in an anomalous centrifuge between bad luck and good fortune and found themselves in the years following their original prescription of olanzapine in the biggest lawsuit ever filed against the pharmaceutical industry and one of the most prepotent corporate lawsuits ever filed in global history. Mossman writes in his article regarding the lawsuit:

> In addition to the "quasi-class action" settlement just described, olanzapine recipients have also filed a number of non "class action" lawsuits, alleging products liability claims centered on Lilly's failure to warn about the drug's harmful side effects. For instance, Lilly settled 18,000 lawsuits for $500 million in early 2007, bringing the total at that timeto "at least $1.2 billion [paid] to 28,500 people who said they were injured by [the] drug." Lilly settled another 900 individual user suits later that year.

One could state this unfortunate occurrence in the off-label usages, side effects, and ineffective precautions taken in regards to olanzapine as a careless or even an absentminded mistake on the part of Eli Lilly and Company, the manufacturer of olanzapine, or Zyprexa. This statement would be unjust. Eli Lilly and Company took necessary precautions to freeze over or black out the harmful effects of olanzapine before it even went into its production stages. The reality is that Eli Lilly and Company deceived their investors and stockholders to ensure the production of olanzapine and the acceptance and implementation of olanzapine by the FDA and in the mental health offices around the world. Those affected by the side effects of olanzapine were not the only people who filed lawsuits against Eli Lilly and Company. Mossman writes:

> In addition to recipients and purchasers of SGAs, shareholders in pharmaceutical companies are potentially affected by extensive and costly litigation. In 2007, Lilly shareholders sued the corporation in the Eastern District of New York for its behavior regarding olanzapine. The shareholders alleged violations of the Securities Exchange Act of 1934 (SFA) §10(b), and the Securities and Exchange Commission's Rule 10b-5, which the SEC created to enforce §10(b); these provisions relate to shareholder communication. Under Rule 10b-5, it is "unlawful for any person, directly or indirectly," to employ a mechanism to defraud, make untrue statements of material facts, omit material facts that would make a statement no longer misleading, or engage in an act that "would operate as fraud or deceit upon any person...." Nonetheless, Rule 10b-5 is only applicable to shareholder communications that were made "in connection with the purchase or sale of any security."

The investors and shareholders prevailed in the lawsuit and Eli Lilly and Company were deemed to have deceived, defrauded, and mislead their investors and shareholders to guarantee the

SGA's surfacing in the pharmaceutical industry and in the universe of mental illness. Mossman goes on: "The crux of this lawsuit was a claim that Lilly misrepresented olanzapine's side effects to shareholders through its marketing campaigns. The suit also claimed that Lilly marketed olanzapine for uses that were not FDA approved in violation of FDA marketing regulations." The perceptive reader might ask the following question. How did this SGA pass preliminary stages in production let alone proceed through the FDA exams and turn out to be well and in order? The answer is simple on paper but the execution of such an act takes sneakiness and disloyalty. The answer: bribery directed not only toward investors and shareholders but also toward FDA officials and even physicians.

The fact is olanzapine, or Zyprexa gained momentum when it should not have. This was made possible by the utilization of Eli Lilly and Company's limitless monetary surplus. As stated, not only investors and shareholders were paid off but also the mental health professionals, who spoke out on the good outcomes of olanzapine, or Zyprexa at conventions and other social gatherings to which mental health professionals gravitate, as speakers and promoters subject to what the pharmaceutical corporations call promotion techniques. This, too, is stated in the Mossman article:

> The promotion techniques used by drag reps and pharmaceutical companies have received substantial publicity over the past few years. Pharmaceutical companies also have employed physicians in various promotional capacities, including efforts to

encourage forms of off-label prescribing that those physicians believe are effective. Physicians are often needed to assist pharmaceutical companies in the development of their products, but they have served as spokespersons for products, too. Accepting this role—often by becoming a member of a company's "speaker's bureau"—and acceptingpayments from pharmaceutical companies is not illegal for physicians, but these "entanglements" are actually "common in the medical industry" and appear to have compromised medical education.

It seems to be the case that when money is involved there comes an innate or attached bias when taking into account the decision making faculties, or reason. Blindness tends to overcome and surface in the populace's thought pool and as Mossman states in regards to the pharmaceutical industry compromise medical education. This form of terrorism utilizes and implements in the mental health professional's psychology a rudimentary and human mechanism which is called positive reinforcement and which is proven to be a source of incentive. However, the mental health professional sees not that his or her opinions are opinions with which the pharmaceutical industry are tampering. Mossman depicts this manipulation in his article:

> Medical schools were once relatively insulated from the influence and lure of pharmaceutical money. But as other sources of funding for research and education have dried up, financial entanglements

have tied many academic doctors to drug companies. By and large, academic recipients of drug companies' largesse do not see their relationships with the industry as influencing their professional activities or biasing their training, particularly if the gifts are small. Apparently, drug companies are savvier, and know that small gifts influence behavior even when the gifts are not linked to explicit requests.

The gifts are intended not to establish good relations with the mental health professional but are intended to change their preferences in the drugs they prescribe to their patients. The gifts are not ones of good relations but as a means for the corporation to establish dominance in the mental health professional's offices. This idea is mentioned also by Dr. Jerome P. Kassirer in the Mossman article:

> Figures from Minnesota, for instance, revealed that psychiatrists who received more than $5,000 from SGA manufacturers wrote more prescriptions of the drugs for children than did other psychiatrists. As Dr. Jerome P. Kassirer, a professor at the Tufts University School of Medicine, commented in an article from ABC News: "'One important question: why would the drug industry spend so much money advertising if they didn't think they were influencing physicians? The notion that this is all for physician education is nonsense.'"

The influence does not stop on the graduation date of medical students nor does it stop at any time throughout their medical career. In fact, the influence, or gift giving by the pharmaceutical corporations begins at the very beginning of students' medical school pursuits and affect them with permanence and with indefiniteness. It is just a matter of which corporation gets to them first. Mossman writes in regards to medical students and gift giving, or bribery:

> Gift-giving by pharmaceutical companies affects future medical professionals as well. A 2005 study published in the Journal of American Medical Association concluded that medical students were "at risk for unrecognized influence by marketing efforts." In reaching that conclusion, the study revealed an average of one sponsored activity attended or one gift received per week, per student. Additionally, the study found that: Most students perceive that they are entitled to gifts. Many simultaneously think that sponsored educational events are likely to be biased, but are helpful. Most think that their prescribing is not likely to be influenced by these interactions and that their colleagues are more likely to be influenced.

The dispersal of gifts and bribes seems to be uncontrolled by law enforcement or any authority on a nationwide level. Influence, money, and the corporations which house all the power on a national and global level in regards to medicine are able to pursue any means of attaining more money, more influence, and more power. They have not been scrutinized on a level or by a people who can compete with their monetary influence and power. Corporate actions are subject to an attribute possessed by all corporations which are a part of the pharmaceutical industry called omnipotence.

The pharmaceutical industry and its long reach and subsidiaries end not only within its own boundaries. In fact, the pharmaceutical industry is involved with social and economic trials and feats, legal and illegal, throughout the globe; the pharmaceutical industry's knowledge of this effectual byproduct which is in all virtuality invisible and which is quite criminalistic in nature can be called money laundering. Some call it the very source of organized criminalistic funding around the world. P. Lilley writes in his book titled *The Untold Truth About Global Money Laundering, International Crime and Terrorism* how this pursuit known as money laundering works in its intimacies, how and why companies launder money, and how organizations like radical terrorists groups in Arabia and drug cartels in central and south America benefit from a seeming commonplace business venture. The companies comprising the pharmaceutical industry are in no way innocent or exempt of this rather traitorous business strategy. Lilley writes in the preface of his book:

> The vast majority of relevant illegal acts are perpetrated to achieve one thing: money. If money is generated by crime, it is useless until original tainted source of funds can be disguised or preferably obliterated. Thus, the dynamic of money

laundering lies at the corrupt heart of many of the
social and economic problems experienced across
the globe. (xii)

The industry in question, that is the pharmaceutical industry, is
by all means one of the most active in this all too relevant and
tainted resource for terrorist groups. How the terrorist groups
such as the Columbian and Mexican cartels, Asian triad gang
networks, and Middle Eastern fundamental terrorists arrive
at such material gains from corporate America and other
corporations around the world, too, will be expounded upon
below. But, per happenstance the term otherwise known as
"dirty money" should be defined with further clarity, that is
money which needs to be laundered in order to protect and
maintain lawful security on the part of corporations, or in this
case pharmaceutical companies.

> Dirty money comes from every kind of criminal
> activity on a global basis. As we see later... this
> includes, but certainly is not limited to: the drugs
> (illegal narcotic trade); illegal arms trading; illegal
> sex business; corruption; fraud; forgery; armed
> robberies; blackmail; extortion; arts and antique
> fraud; internet fraud; smuggling; tax fraud; and
> trafficking in human beings. (xiii)

We have well established that companies like Lily which are
now recovering from multi-million dollar lawsuits and which
have perpetrated in the market of prescription medication a
faulty and harmful drug are guilty of not all but some of the
above corporate and criminalistic activity from corruption to

forgery to fraud but well have their hands in all of the above organized and criminalistic activities. Whether they know of their participation in organized crime throughout the world is of no importance. Their washing money and their shipping billions of dollars overseas to protect their business ethics is a running and fluidic effect which fills in the cracks of otherwise codependent criminalistic organizations. The reliance of corporate crime and corporate America on the part of criminalistic organizations around the world has been quite prevalent in ongoing investigations by U.S. law enforcement and has been a question poised by many politicians, law enforcement officers, and authors alike. Lilley in his book *The Untold Truth About Global Money Laundering, International Crime and Terrorism* which scrutinizes the finite aspects of terrorist funding via corporate crime, has created a comprehensive contribution to ongoing corporate literature. He states in the very beginning of his book that:

> Since 9/11, this topic has become strongly linked to money laundering. [The following] hopefully provides an evaluation of why it is very dangerous to confuse terrorist funding and money laundering. Traditional ideas on money laundering do not apply to terrorist financing. The basis of criminal money laundering involves washing large amounts of dirty money. However, terrorist funding can and does operate on a shoestring. (xv-xvi)

That terrorist funding descends a long chain of command beginning from honest taxpayers and ailed individuals who need medication and who pay for medicine, then into the corporate bank accounts, and then through offshore bank accounts, illegitimate and invisible money holders into the bank accounts of criminal organizations around the world is not an invalid statement. In fact, as Lilley puts it, it is quite evident as per techniques used by these corporations to wash their hands of fraudulent monies and operates much like a Newton's cradle apparatus, one metal ball striking on one end a series of conductors and the ball, or entity on the opposite end benefits with kinetic energy. As well as manipulative business tactics in the placement of funds corporations also use techniques such as money siphoning and rounding down when it comes to gross profit and quarterly results. Anand Adkihari states in his article "How Funds are Siphoned" regarding money siphoning and monetary manipulation on a corporate level that, "The project cost is generally inflated by 20-30 per cent by conniving with vendors or suppliers of plant and machineries to take the money out from the company." The inflation of funds required to create in this case a new drug, the rounding down of internal figure projections, inflated funds directed toward outsourcing, sales and distribution, and consultancy and advisory payments are implemented to reach the uppermost limit of their budget and expenditure in order to ensure equal or even higher funding from investors, shareholders, and even government subsidiary funds in the next quarter or fiscal year—a well-known strategy used by not only the corporate industry but also the collegiate system, public and centralized government departments, the Vatican and just as well any other organization who has implemented and is operating on a limited, if one could call it as so, budget. In fact, these budgets are mere means to acquire more funds in the following quarter or fiscal year and are quite the façade when attempting to accrue not only funds but public and private favor. Lilley goes on to write in regards to the detrimental effects of corporate money laundering and unfortunate business ethics that:

> Entire countries have been brought to their knees by criminal activity and the requirement to convert the resultant ill-gotten gains into a universally acceptable currency (which is predominantly US dollars). Colombia is an obvious example; Mexico is fast approaching the same situation. Elsewhere in South America, in Bolivia 300,000 citizens are involved either indirectly or directly in the coca business, and the eliminations of half of the producing fields in recent years has significantly contributed to unemployment and poverty. In Russia, the influence of criminal groupings is all pervasive from street level to the upper echelons of the Kremlin itself. In Burma, it is widely believed that the military junta itself is involved in drug trafficking—and this country is merely one of a group of suspected 'narco states'. (2)

Illegitimate organizations in Latin America and abroad are the same as so called legitimate organizations in the United States but the legitimate organization in question here, the pharmaceutical industry, has backing it a fear of sickness and a dependency which is understandable when regarding terminal sicknesses. The illegal drug trade and the pharmaceutical industry are polar opposites, or reflections of one another both of which enact similar if not the same criminalistic acts including but not limited to corruption, fraud, forgery, blackmail, internet fraud, and tax fraud as is the case in the olanzapine, or Zyprexa lawsuit. This is only one syphilic instant that got caught in the net. The superordinate pharmaceutical industry in America and around the globe like the coca issue in Bolivia mentioned above fortifies a snaring unemployment problem and maintains poverty in lower- and middle-class families around the globe as per its tumorous presence which is malignant and which has in recent decades metastasized into more direct routes and into more significant nodes regarding criminalistic funding and corporate-familial-terrorist triangulation, or codependence. It has been proven that this monetary flow is evident and self-sustaining. Lilley writes when taking into account the billions of dollars which cannot be legitimated on home soil that, "The massive sums of money generated by such activity need to be legitimized by inserting and washing them in international banking and business systems" (2). One could go so far as to state an even more intricate and interwoven state of sustainability insofar as the pharmaceutical industry, organized crime around the globe, and ailed individuals in need of medicine. The sustainability which is perpetual and may as well be called eternal is in fact comprised of six titular points: 1) the organized crime syndicates who revolve and survive on corporate fraud and illegal trade, 2) the pharmaceutical industry and just as well any other multi-billion dollar industry, 3) fundamental terrorist groups, 4) governmental inactivity as a façade, 5) internal organizations which are corruptible and which are supposed international law enforcement, 6) the citizenry, or in this case the sick or mental ill used as a life support system, or legitimizing entity—all of these components make a Magen Dawid of an entity which is sustainable in itself and which circulates monetary funds on an eternal and systematized basis.

It has been stated by Lilley in his book that terrorist groups are funded by a variety of sources including:

donations;

the use of charities and non-profit organizations;

front companies;

state sponsorship;

fraud;

smuggling;

the narcotics trade;

blackmail and protection rackets;

corruption;

counterfeiting;

other criminal activities

But, he goes further in his description of terrorist funding by creating and separating the two types of terrorist groups, differentiating them by their main sources of reliance. Lilley writes that:

> The US Treasury Department observes that 'terrorist groups in Europe, East Asia and Latin America rely on common criminal activities such as extortion, kidnapping, the narcotics trade, counterfeiting, and fraud. Middle Eastern groups rely on commercial enterprises, donations and funds skimmed from charities.' (137-8)

These groups and with certainty the latter of the two groups mentioned above legitimize their war crimes with religion. Spiritual and religious advanced individuals who are the means of contextualization when reading this book are the constituency, or the infinitesimal filaments of this supposed validating idea which in all reality is a stretch for validation made by fundamental terrorists and which is called organized religion.

The olanzapine, or Zyprexa case is only one of the instances which have been caught by the greater populace and which have been tainted in its motives and practices from their very conceptions. Pharmaceutical lawsuits are in progress at present but mere monetary compensation for physical, mental, and even spiritual intrusiveness on the part of hasty, criminalistic, and blasphemous pharmaceutical corporations are not just when taking into account the literal endlessness of their profiteering and pestilent dispositions.

LIFE AFTER SCHIZOPHRENIA

I do not take at face value anything set before me and that is a good attribute and a bad attribute, a pro and also a con, as I see it. Nor do I take at face value what I read. This includes forms of literature from non-fiction to religious texts. It is the case, however, that wisdom can be found in the words on a page from comic strips to historical texts. Timeless parables, however, and wisdom found in such texts as *Rig Veda* and even in biblical verses are worthy of recognition. In this regard, all are between Scylla and Charybdis and while I myself was speculating on including such an idiom it is quite relevant to the present state of interpersonal relations, familial and otherwise, monetary and intellectual investments, and the corporate and legislative conundrum which is all too prevalent. The common element in all read and written, created and destroyed, believed and rejected are the intentions and motivations when initiating any given operation. Intentions and motivations as we have established thus far in this book differ and are quite drastic in difference at that, in all fields which are split by two or more opposing belief systems. Differences in intentions and motivations are quite prevalent in the mental health universe in particular. The separation between the mental health professional's aspiration for utopia, the misdiagnosed schizophrenic patient's longing for self-actualization, and the pharmaceutical industry's insatiable starvation for money, influence, and the power that comes along with money and influence is radical in its triangularity. It seems as though the yin and yang, that is the counterintuitive manifestation of so called psychotic symptoms and the misdiagnosed patients themselves, are rotating and oscillating into pansophism which is the ultimate goal of the individual in his or her time on earth and which is the primary aim of humanity as a singular and sovereign entity.

Schizophrenia and the Spiritual Nature of the Human

———

THE FINAL ESSAY IN this book is the one which you are now reading and which is concerned with the tripartition of trends of delusions experienced by the schizophrenic patient in conjunction with Jungian psychology of the soul and religion. It is the case that many individuals diagnosed, or misdiagnosed with schizophrenia have thoughts and ideas pertaining to religion-oriented ideology and to self-actualization on levels which are prerequisite to atonement with the subconscious and which more times rather than not are called delusions of grandeur. The issues of concern in this essay also regards the surfacing of the subconscious in the so called schizophrenic individual and populace, the acquisition and preservation of soul as used in Jungian terminology, and historical, literary, and scientific texts in relation to these psychological and quite valid theories. There comes a time in many individuals' lives when the question dawns, arising or conjured from the depths of human thought and emotion, which has the individual recapitulating his or her life at present and evoking memories, to validate his or her present state of mind, belief systems, and decisions. This rising of self-scrutiny is inevitable and could be called a circumvention of sorts of brain essences, retrospection regarding physical ailments and past and present revelations, and even notions regarding such ethereal and removed concepts like reincarnation; an entire book can be written on these matters of similitude between brain functions, memory, spirituality and religiosity, the simplicity of physical ailments and revelations, and the intimate notion of reincarnation—all of which will not be discussed in depth here. Instead, the verbalized ideas of the misfortunate schizophrenic patient and the theories, like schizophrenia, which make their so called delusions of grandeur a state of illness and not ideas of introspection, spirituality, and religiosity, all of which are ideas worthy of scrutiny, will be discussed. These so called delusions of grandeur, or introspective ideas are all society at large has to empathize with supposed psychotic individuals. As is the thematic undertone of this book, the apprehension of self and soul while a part of the schizophrenic universe will be set before the reader in a practical sense and may well shift ideologies of those affected by schizophrenia, patient and family alike and even the mental health professional, into a locale of more traditional methods of psychological adaptation regarding so called symptoms of schizophrenia.

The tight-fitted connection between religious or spiritual intuition, the perception of sounds and optical sensations, and the misconstrued ideologies which entail mental healthiness will, too, be discussed. While many individuals who verbalize their experiences with metaphysical and supernatural exchanges tend to be donned psychotic and are institutionalized, the issue of justification, or validity is in question when looking at the metaphysical and supernatural exchanges through tradition and old-world ideologies. Tradition, the metaphysical, and the supernatural insofar as their semblance with the mind and soul has come to a frank end as of the emergence of antipsychotic medication and the hysteria of disorder rather than order in the contemporary era. That being said, the analysis of the three types of delusions most prevalent in supposed schizophrenic patients will be looked at from two polar opposite points, that is the point of view of the spiritual and religious advanced individual and the point of view of the mental health professional. Dziwota and associates in their article titled, "On the border of deep spirituality and psychosis... a case study" go through the three types of delusions and deem them the rudiments of the metaphysical world of the schizophrenic patient. The first type of delusion considers, as Dziwota and associates have donned it, the ontological trend, that is the actualization of a world filled with mysterious energies, cosmic moral struggles, et cetera as the first type of schizophrenic delusion. Dziwota and associates write:

> The metaphysical world of a schizophrenic patient revolves around three main trends: ontological, eschatological and charismatic. The ontological trend is a turn towards the fantasy and magic of a world imbued with mysterious energies, the forces of good and evil, as well as waves penetrating human thoughts and behavior. The perception of a patient with schizophrenia is characterized by the fact that they see anything as filled with divine or satanic substance.

The supposed schizophrenic individual experiencing this type of so called delusion can be called an observer of morality with the notion of the cosmos at the periphery. The perception that everything is filled with divine or satanic substance is a notion that goes back to the Crusades in 1099 and even prior the Crusades, a world which was composed of the Roman Empire in the west, the Muslim entities in the east, and Byzantium in the middle, flanked on both sides by the Roman Empire and the Muslim entities. The notion of holiness and righteousness has been carried throughout the history of man up until the mid-twentieth century when the technological boom took place, neuroscience having been conceived and developed, and a transference of faith having occurred from spirituality and religiosity to what one could call synthetic knowledge, ending at once traditional perceptions.

The notion of mysterious energies and waves penetrating human thoughts and behavior, too, has in the youth gained momentum over the recent years. It seems to be the case that the believability of these notions and their being determined as delusional take place within family circles and in circles of close companionship with those experiencing this religious intuition together with a dash of ill-composure, ill enough to raise questions and incite the search for a mental health professional. I must extrapolate the notion of western medicine and ideology versus eastern medicine and ideology. The concepts of energies, morality, and divinity are much more accepted and are even revered in countries and regions in the east. Here, in the westernized and scientific hogwash-minded concern for individuals experiencing metaphysical and supernatural realizations, energies, morality, and divinity are dejected ideologies. The westernized ideologies are rather a disgrace from supposed schizophrenic patients' points of view. On the part of the mental health professional, however, the administration, prescription, and systematic and successive shift of belief systems in the schizophrenic patients are a shot at utopia which too is a disgrace on the part of psychological and psychiatric tradition and foundations and which is a rather stark attempt at removing possible futures of self-actualization and self-preservation in misdiagnosed schizophrenic individuals.

As stated by Dziwota and associates, the second trend in supposed schizophrenic delusions regards the apocalypse. Dziwota and associates write:

> The eschatological trend, in turn, is mainly related to issues like the end of the world, the ultimate purpose of man, etc. The image of the end of the world might be more or less apocalyptic—either it is limited to the patient's immediate family or encompasses the entire globe. In schizophrenia, the catastrophic mood reaches a climax, which is preceded by a state of apprehension—the world becomes very mysterious; the anxiety increases.

The tantamount aspect of this trend of delusion which makes spiritual and religious advanced individuals vulnerable, as stated in the first trend of delusion, is ill-composure, or as Dziwota and associates write a state of apprehension. An empathic, spiritual and religious advanced individual, empathic to the world around him or her and perceptive of the goings on insofar as current events and actual trends in global and national politics cannot be called delusional as per notions of terminableness, or as some might state it apocalypse. Yet, they are called delusional. The term apocalypse is an extreme, or radical term to use but the association between the spiritual and religious advanced individuals' intuitions and the notion of deludedness has been contrived by the mental health professional and not by the schizophrenic or spiritual and religious advanced individual. As is thematic in the case of the mental health professional and his or her rationale behind the diagnosing of individuals as schizophrenic and the prescribing of antipsychotic medications and the implementation of institutionalization and observation, all rooted in the mental health professional's perception of what is best for the individual at hand who is experiencing metaphysical and supernatural exchanges, for society as a whole as per these individuals' beliefs and behaviors, and the idealistic utopian society which goes hand in hand with the efforts of redirecting belief systems and fate, the forcible efforts exacted by the mental health professional, are quite detrimental. While those misdiagnosed with schizophrenia are in fact quite serene the conception of them at large is that they are volatile in their personalities and behaviors. But, what has not been put into question is the causation of such supposed volatility as per Jungian psychology and the paradox, or juxtaposition of titular associations and their succeeding thoughts and behaviors, a question which will be discussed in this essay.

LIFE AFTER SCHIZOPHRENIA

The third and final trend of delusion as accepted by the mental health professional regards charisma, or a high sense of self on the part of the so called schizophrenic individual in their relation to the people and the society around them. This is the type of delusion in which individuals profess they are messianic or possessed by demons or by prominent figures in history. Dziwota and associates write:

> The charismatic trend, as understood by Kepiński, is associated with the fact that the patient, who is in the central position of the world, feels immortal, immaterial, almighty, as either God or Satan; the fate of the entire world depends on them. They are endowed with holiness, divinity, Satanism; they live their entire life under the sign of a gift charisma.

This is a peculiar trend of delusion and far more difficult to justify. But, it can be justified by putting into perspective the subliminal and subconscious nodes of thought which have become manifest over the course of human history such as political figures, musicians, writers, patron saints, and many other different kinds of notable individuals which have receded on temporal levels into the subconscious of man. The macrocosm which resides in the subconscious of man can be communicable and can send signals to the forefront of a man or woman's thoughts as suggestions, or preliminary steps toward pansophism. This is the case with individuals experiencing this type of supposed delusional trend. However, their claim that they are messianic or possessed by any notable figure in the history of man is not accurate as per the name of the notable figure with whom the supposed delusional individual has made contact and the actual patient-historical figure affiliation in all reality. It is easy to see why the mental health professional does not believe in such metaphysical and supernatural communication. The mental health professional as most individuals alive in the western hemisphere have not even considered such possibilities of subconscious-conscious communication and self-actualization and self-preservation mechanisms which are in fact quite natural.

The intercommunication between the subconscious and the conscious minds is the exact notion off of which Carl Gustav Jung based his theories on the human psychology and religion in his book titled *Psychology and Religion*. He starts off by stating the same notion I have suggested above, that is the cognizance of an internal and mental transposition of cues and symbols through the mind or brain in a form known as telegraphy which is defined as the telegraphing of code or symbols from one locale to another. Telegraphy, however, is not the only means used by the subconscious to communicate with its forefront or conscious and aware compatriot. Synchronicity in occurrences which seem coincidental, or freakish to the incognizant individual is a semblance taking place between the subconscious and conscious, micro- and macro-level cosmology in the spiritual and religious advanced individual. The frequent observation of such telegraphy or synchronicity builds momentum like a ball, or a tire rolling down a graded plane and further advances the perceptions and mental faculties of the spiritual and religious advanced individuals. The diagnosis, or misdiagnosis of schizophrenia, however, impedes this naturalistic ability in pansophical inclinations and in some cases even kills the ability it total. The subconscious and its nodes which are composed of said historical figures, historical events, and even seeming randomized artwork are that sensitive to influences like the aforementioned transference of faith and belief systems regarding the human mind, brain, and the origins of existence. As Carl Gustav Jung states, "A neurosis is a humiliating defeat and is felt as such by people who are not entirely unconscious of their own psychology" (8-9). This preliminary statement in Jung's *Psychology and Religion* opens up for discussion his theory regarding the subconscious-conscious mind and religion, the mind's symbology, and dreams which are covered in the 130 some odd pages in the book and which are covered with more brevity in this one.

Put forth in the first two essays in this book are the validity of neurological bases and neurological deviation as causes to supposed mental illness, in specific schizophrenia. The arbitrary and foolish observations made between Rodentia and the schizophrenic individual are not only arbitrary and foolish but rather hasty and leave the entirety of neuroscience and the neuroscientist's validity in question. The gestalt psychology of these neurologists and mental health professionals are attempts at justifying a condition which was conceived by and of themselves and with a rather stark disregarding of tradition and all former collected knowledge regarding the mind, man, and metaphysics and the supernatural. As Carl Gustav Jung puts it:

The un-deniable connection between psyche and brain gives this point of view a certain strength, but not enough to make it an unshakable truth. We do not know whether there is a real disturbance of the organic processes of the brain in a case of neurosis, and if there are disorders of an endocrine nature it is impossible to say whether they are not effects rather than causes (10).

This is an observation which has been bypassed in contemporary sciences. The suggestion made by Carl Gustav Jung is that the supposed deviant neuroscience, or neurosis as he calls it may well be effects of a subconscious change, or emergence of former latent thoughts, abilities, and intuitive faculties rather than the cause of supposed hallucinations and delusions i.e. subconscious-conscious communication and the expansion of the mind into otherworld locales. One cannot deny, however, that individuals who are experiencing abnormal thoughts act and are composed in, one could say, an eccentric way. Many times, the communication between the subconscious and the conscious mind, the expansion of the mind into otherworld locales can be detrimental to the individual, in some cases for a limited period of time and in other cases on a chronic level. The notable historical figures, timeless events in history, and other universal truths in the mind of man have as stated receded into the subconscious of the human mind over time and are subject to an almost animalistic, or visceral susceptibility which Sigmund Freud calls the ID and which the Iroquois tribe of North America calls the Great Peacemaker, or Skennenrahawi Deganawida.

But, the donning of this force, or entity with a name in many cases and in especial cases when the search for contemporary mental health interaction is rooted out is quite fruitless. In regards to this subconscious force, entity, or entities Carl Gustav Jung writes while referring to a case study of a so called psychotic individual:

> They grow out of the unconscious mind and invade consciousness with their weird and unassailable convictions and impulses. Our patient's case belonged in the latter category. Despite his culture and intelligence, he was a helpless victim of something which obsessed or possessed him. He was utterly unable to help himself in any way against the demoniacal power of his morbid idea. It overgrew him indeed like a carcinoma. One day the idea had appeared and from then on it remained unshakably; there were only short free intervals. The existence of such cases explains, to a certain extent, why people are afraid of becoming conscious of themselves. There might really be something behind the screen—one never knows—and thus people prefer "to take into account and to observe carefully" factors external to their consciousness. In most people, there is a sort of primitive δεισιδαιμονία concerning the possible contents of the unconscious. Beyond all natural shyness, shame and tact, there is a secret fear of the unknown "perils of the soul." Of course, one is reluctant to admit such a ridiculous fear. But one should realize that thisfear

> is by no means unjustifiable; on the contrary, it is
> only too well founded. We arenever sure that a new
> idea will not seize either upon ourselves or upon our
> neighbors. (14-15)

The consideration of the rudimentary human emotion fear is called into question in the above quotation and does bring forth with immediacy the semblance between the subconscious and the conscious minds and, as Carl Gustav Jung puts it, the primitive δεισιδαιμονία which is Greek and, translated into English, means something like the low demon. The morbid idea which surfaced in the mind of this individual in this case study is a common effect of the type of cognizance being discussed, that is an acknowledgment or realization of the self. The curious sense one experiences upon the acknowledging, feeling or even seeing their subconscious is quite intertwined with heightened senses like paranoia and euphoria and are deemed psychotic in nature by the mental health professional who proceeds to medicate and even institutionalize the individual who is experiencing this natural and quite privileged exchange with his or her subconscious, or his or her self in entirety. In fact, the medication, institutionalization, and chastising of these individuals who are experiencing rare human phenomenon can be called a crime against humanity though not many see it as so. The omnipresent entity that is the subconscious mind in most individuals' points of view is unconscious, or nonexistent. The primitive or otherworld aspects of the mind and self, or identity are not acknowledged nor are they sensed by most individuals. Yet, the subconscious is conscious in and of itself and it does take a role in the everyday occurrences and actions surrounding every individual every single day. The subconscious makes itself known as stated through semblance in nature and in dreams, and also other more supernatural ways which I will not get into at present. The conscious entity which thrives unknown in the minds of men and women changes and manipulates the world for its host, if you will, depending on the benevolence or malevolence present in the individual at his or her depths. While many mysterious occurrences such as the perceiving of auditory and optical phenomenon take place many unfortunate occurrences, too, which surface as notions from the subconscious take place on a corporeal level such as increased violent behaviors and euthanasia. This is a battle within the individual but also a battle quite present between contemporary theories of mind and brain and the naturalistic minds of man on cephalocaudal and even proximodistal levels, that is head-phallus and core-extremity levels. Contemporary theories and traditional theories in the subconscious mind compete with ceaselessness. The struggle taking place between the two extremes, as depicted in the second essay herein which is titled "Schizophrenia and its Devout Perpetrators" and which discusses the characteristics and elements of belief systems, widens the divide and makes a hazardous fissure in the very rudiments of man. Carl Gustav Jung states in his *Psychology and Religion* that:

> We know from modern as well as from ancient history that such ideas can be rather strange, so peculiar, indeed, that not everybody can agree with them. The result may be that all dissenters, no

matter how well meaning or reasonable they are, get
burnt alive or have their heads cut off or are disposed
of in masses by the more modern machine gun. (15)

Such was the case with Galileo Galilei as earlier depicted. It
seems to be the case that the tumultuous striving for mental
health is rather non-linear as per the constant and subsequent
back and forth between ridicule directed toward so called
schizophrenic individuals and the outward acts of hostility
committed by them. This chaotic interaction which in many
cases goes unforeseen is further depicted by Carl Gustav Jung
in the context of the ancient Egyptian myth, the Epic of
Gilgamesh, an Akkadian poem in correlation with
contemporary and unlearned themes which are prevalent
throughout the myth and which are relevant to contemporary
schizophrenic, for the lack of better term, delusions. Jung
writes:

> When in the Babylonian Epos Gilgamesh's
> arrogance and mean freaking ways defy the gods,
> they invent and create a man equal in strength to
> Gilgamesh in order to check the hero's unlawful
> ambition. The very same thing has happened to our
> patient: he is athinker who has settled, or is always
> going to settle, the world by the power of his
> intellect and reason. His ambition has at least
> succeeded in carving his own personal fate. He has
> forced everything under the inexorable law of his
> reason, but somewhere nature escaped and came
> back with a vengeance in the form of perfectly

unassailable nonsense, the cancer idea. This clever device was formed by the unconscious mind to keep him on a merciless and cruel leash. It was the worst blow which could be given to all his reasonable ideals and above all to his belief in the all-powerful human will. Such an obsession can only occur in a person who makes a habitual misuse of reason and intellect for an egotistical power purpose. Gilgamesh, however, escaped the revenge of the gods. He had warning dreams to which he paid attention. They showed him how he could overcome his foe. Our patient, living in an age where the gods have become extinct and are even in bad repute, also had such dreams, but he did not listen to them. How could an intelligent man be so superstitious as to take dreams seriously! The very common prejudice against dreams is but one of the symptoms of a far more serious undervaluation of the human soul in general. The marvelous development of science and technics has been counterbalanced on the other side by an appalling lack of wisdom and introspection. It is true that our religious teaching speaks of an immortal soul; but it has very few kind words for the actual human psyche, which would go straight to eternal damnation if it were not for a special act of Divine Grace. Those two important factors are largely responsible for the general undervaluation of the psyche, but not entirely. Much older than those

> relatively recent developments are the primitive fear
> of and aversion to everything that borders on the
> unconscious (18-19).

This rather lengthy quotation has incorporated the essential components of the human soul and its preservation which is the theme of the Epic of Gilgamesh, an Akkadian poem and which is the theme of the book you are now reading. Dreams are the foremost way for the subconscious to communicate with the individual who are not as of yet perceptive on a level to observe and even conjure semblance in their surroundings. In this regard, dreams are the device used to actualize and preserve the soul. The roots, or origins of identity in an individual is the soul in its entirety. The donning of an individual who is having so called unexplainable, metaphysical, supernatural, spiritual and religious experiences as schizophrenic is a damaging monstrosity imposed on a given individual's soul. This, of course, is deduced from the Jungian approach to psychology and religion, and in effect the soul. Finding two groups of people who agree on the origins and intimacies of the soul and the psychology of religion is near impossible. Ask a priest what is the soul and where it comes from and he will tell you his interpretation of the soul from an existential point of view. Ask a musician, or any other artist the origins and intimacies of the soul and he will give you his granted perception. But, we are looking at the soul through the concrete or shall we say sensible circumstances which make the soul and its innate mystery existent, that is the entirety of the above devices used to establish communication between the subconscious and the conscious, from telegraphy to dreaming to semblance in nature. Carl Gustav Jung has suggested when introducing fear in the context of the surfacing of the subconscious a term, "perils of soul." The perils of soul could go on for eternity but in this case, in the discussion of aberrational belief systems and the subsequent fissure in the rudiments of man the most substantial peril of soul as Jung terms it is the "loss of soul," which is defined by Jung as follows:

> One of the "perils of the soul" is, for instance, the loss of a soul. This is a case of a part of the psyche becoming unconscious again. Another example is the amok condition, the equivalent of the berserk condition in the Germanic saga. This is a more or less complete trance, often accompanied by devastating social effects (19).

The receding of the otherworld sensations, the religious intuition, et cetera which have become manifest in the misdiagnosed schizophrenic individual back into the subconscious is as stated above the "loss of soul," or the finality of identity, or self in entirety. The monstrosity which has become for all intents and purposes omnipresent and which has gained momentum as per the transposition of faith and belief systems from tradition and old-world methodology to contemporary neuroscience and gestalt psychology as per the filling in so to speak of absent and essential aspects of the human mind on the part of the contemporary scientist is a subject, or derivation of irrationality. The devastating social effects which Carl Gustav Jung in the year 1966 suggests may occur and which are too prevalent today in the early twenty-first century and also the momentum built in the theory of schizophrenia are effects of the "loss of soul." The "loss of soul" in question, however, as per devastating social effects are not a loss of soul on an individualistic level, not in entirety, but a loss of soul on a sociological and racial level, racial not in ethnicity but in humanity and in the pansophical entity which lies in the subconscious and which is surfacing with more and more frequency and with more and more erroneousness. Man is not only a singular term but a term which can be used to encompass the entirety of existence, all spheres of existence from the temporal to the epistemological. When Jung writes on the reintegration of man he speaks not only of the individual man but of man on a universal level:

> He would be a new being, in other words. The patient has to undergo an important change through the reintegration of his hitherto split-off instinctivity, and is thus to be made over into a new man. The modern mind has forgotten those old truths that speak of the death of the old man and of the making of a new one, of spiritual rebirth and similar old-fashioned "mystical absurdities." (41)

These instances of spiritual rebirth and similar old-fashioned mystical absurdities occur in some cases in subtle ways and in some cases in outlandish, temporal ways. To believe in the assumption that a notion, minuscule or absurd, is an effect of a predisposed mental illness or schizophrenia is to espouse hereticalness in the finite intimacies of man and also his contrivances which include the contemporary sciences. A dependence on supposed epistemological superiority, that is the mental health professional and just as well any social respectable status in any given universe is, too, omnipresent and gaining momentum with rapidity. The preservation of the individualist is at hand. The schizophrenic ideologies which permeate throughout the global populace are voiding human intellectualism, religiosity, and humanism. The finality of tradition, classical methodologies, and genuine knowledge is enamored by a synthesis of pseudo-intellectualism and naïveté. It may have already occurred. If tradition is dead and if classical methodologies have been replaced by synthetic faith and if genuine knowledge has been solvated by an ill-motivated network of technology the subconscious, its origins, and man in his totality have been blotted out. Nevertheless, 98% of people on earth dream. A median of 17% of people on earth hear voices that other people do not hear. The conflagration which has taken the globe and the faith of the western populace and which is known as schizophrenia must be controlled—it must be contained to prevent the scorching of the virile, spiritual and religious advanced individual—and then man with the punctual arrival and recognition of the subconscious mind from which such "mystical absurdities" surface can procure the consummation of man on an individualistic and on a wholesome level and apprehend life after schizophrenia.

Conclusion

———

THE PRECEDING ESSAYS all find themselves in a final, or terminal context which incorporates the actualization and preservation of the soul. Many times, those misdiagnosed with schizophrenia lose the context in which they first had otherworld, supernatural, or deviant thoughts. In a sense, this is a loss not only of creativity, inspiration, individuality, and identity but also divinity and soul. One could argue there is no greater loss to a man or a woman. The preceding essays were written with the pretext of schizophrenia in mind but can be applied to just as well any other epistemological and performative categorization from race to sexuality to nationalism to religious affiliation to class and even habitual inclinations—any or all categorization which has associated with it misfortunate stigmata. No matter which epistemological or performative category one belongs to the dichotomous reality-actuality perception of existence, the five spheres of existence—epistemological, performative, spatial, corporeal, and temporal spheres—apply. The preconceived or deep embedded belief systems of the bigot can be dismantled by the thirteen characteristics of belief systems and the seven elements of belief systems. Socialization, functionality, interpersonal relations within the family and within the work place as per one's work associates, within the neighborhood and within the socio-economic class to which one belongs, within the groups of friends and acquaintances with whom one interacts on the weekends and evenings all have their exchanges with human defense mechanisms such as sublimation, dismissiveness, and even denial. The multitude of microcosms, or industries to which individuals belong from preferences in music to preferences in food products to preferences or dependence on medication to means of transportation used to get from home to work, work to home, home to supermarket, and supermarket back to home all partake in and implement their effects on the individual on conscious and just as well subconscious levels. All these components—finite pieces of existence and their peculiar affiliations, belief and faith systems, interpersonal and introspective encounters, preferences in consumables and devices and art—create a sense of identity and are active in the consummation of selves to which this book extends insight as far as thematics and to which pansophical cognizance pertains. The essays preceding this conclusion are by no means comprehensive in the identity of man or woman and his or her countless and limitless caches of intellect, creativity, and identity, his or her symbology which have descended through the epochs as oscillating and enumerating entities. This book has in its pages only a partial conception of man and depicts from many a standpoint, as this era is unlike any of its predecessors, his rudiments which are omnipresent and which with good fortune will not be forgotten.

In the shift from toddlerhood to adolescence to adulthood some things go unchanged— cherished memories, musical inclination, and favorite Saturday morning cartoon characters for instance.

LIFE AFTER SCHIZOPHRENIA

Three or four years ago, quite a long while before I made the decision to write this book—and a great many things can happen over the course of a day let alone three or four years—my father and I were deciding what to cook for a family dinner which was a commonplace occurrence in our household but which had not occurred in quite a while as per my siblings' and my own living away at college, an occurrence which would now in fact recur, it being a summer month, the family together, the sunlight and empyrean Florida sky commixing and descending its chromatic and virile wavelengths. Through this, the shimmering and hazy heat rising off the road my father and I drove to the supermarket, collected our ingredients for dinner, and upon standing in the checkout line I saw in the candy rack a peculiar chocolate bar which reminded me with suddenness of my mother who was back at home waiting for our return and which struck me as rather undeniable as per its plumpness and pungent label. It was a Baby Ruth chocolate bar, my mother's favorite chocolate bar, I knew, since her childhood. Knowing already I was going to add the Baby Ruth chocolate bar to our carriage of acquisitions, I said to my father who was in front of me, "Baby Ruth. Why not get that for mom. It is her favorite after all." He turned and saw the Baby Ruth chocolate bar in the candy rack beside us. The plumpness of the Baby Ruth chocolate bar and the pungent label of the Baby Ruth chocolate bar must not have struck him with the same suddenness, and he told me it was all right. It is no big deal. There is no need for it. This, too, struck me with suddenness because a chocolate bar, something so minuscule and even infinitesimal is not a bad idea, not a bad present to buy for a spouse, not a bad present at all. In fact, I rather thought it was a good idea, and I said so. "Buy this for mom," I said. "And tell her you bought it for her and that it was your idea to buy it for her. Do not tell her I told you to buy it for her. She will appreciate it more than you can know." He picked up the Baby Ruth chocolate bar without reluctance and paid for it and then the candy bar went into the plastic shopping bag which we brought out to the car. Then, we were off, homebound, and would be arriving in the driveway within five minutes, the supermarket quite close to our home but what is not close to home in such a small town in the state of Florida?

Once in the kitchen, my father and I unloaded all the plastic shopping bags and put the items in their respective places, expectant of the family dinner which was to occur within two hours. My mother was upstairs. She was not able to hear the conversation between my father and I. Toward the end of the stowing away of foodstuffs I turned to him, the Baby Ruth chocolate bar on the countertop, and said, "Remember. Do not tell her it was me who suggested we buy the chocolate bar for her." And he did remember to withhold the fact that I was the one who had suggested we buy her the chocolate bar and we are all better off because of that. The family dinner went well. All ate well. And by the time the dishes were put into the dish washer and by the time people were relaxing here and there throughout the house, my mother took her Baby Ruth chocolate bar and opened it. She and I were sitting at the kitchen table and she was well.

"Baby Ruth are my favorite chocolate bars," she said. "They always were."

LIFE AFTER SCHIZOPHRENIA

"I know," I said, and we were quiet for many seconds while she took bite after bite of the Baby Ruth chocolate bar.

"This was dad's idea," she said. "At least that's what he says. He says he saw the Baby Ruth and thought of me because he knew it was my favorite candy bar."

"I know," I said. "I was there when he bought it."

"He is so health conscious, though. It is unlike him to buy a candy bar on a whim or for no reason."

"It is," I said.

The dialogue she and I were having would find its way into a manuscript regarding schizophrenia, its misconceptions, and its causes and effects. The manuscript regarding schizophrenia would comprise a theory which I could not have guessed in a hundred years I would be writing and which is now near finished and entitled *Life After Schizophrenia*.

"Strange," she said. "You're sure you had nothing to do with this?" she said. "You didn't tell him to buy this Baby Ruth bar for me, did you?"

"No," I said. "I didn't." But, that was a lie.

References

ADHIKARI, ANAND. HOW Funds are Siphoned. (n.d.).

Retrieved June 01, 2017, from http://www.businesstoday.in/magazine/cover-story/how-funds-are-siphoned/story/3684.html[1]

Bleuler E:

Die Prognose der Dementia præcox (Schizophre-niegruppe). Allgemeine Zeitschrift für Psychiatrie und psychschgerichtliche Medizin 1908; 65:436–464

Bottoms, S. (2014).

Timeless Cruelty: Performing the Stanford Prison Experiment. *Performance Research*, *19*(3), 162-175.

doi:10.1080/13528165.2014.935170

Brown, A. S., & Lau, F. S. (2016).

1. http://www.businesstoday.in/magazine/cover-story/how-funds-are-siphoned/story/3684.html

Chapter 2: A Review of the Epidemiology of Schizophrenia. *Handbook Of Behavioral Neuroscience*, 23 (Modeling the Psychopathological Dimensions of Schizophrenia), 17-30. doi:10.1016/B978-0-12-800981-9.00002-X

de Almeida Campos, M. m., & Gomes, H. h. 2017.

Ontology: Several Theories on the Representation of Knowledge Domains. *Knowledge Organization*, *44*(3), 178-186.

Dziwota, E., Żmuda, D., Dubiel, R., Dziwota, K., Markiewicz, R., Makara-Studzińska, M., & Olajossy, M. (2016).

On the border of deep spirituality and psychosis... A case study. *Current Problems Of Psychiatry*, *17*(3), 183-197. doi:10.1515/cpp-2016-0020

Fusar-Poli, P., & Politi, P. (2008).

Paul Eugen Bleuler and the Birth of Schizophrenia (1908). American Journal of Psychiatry, 165(11), 1407-1407. doi:10.1176/appi.ajp. 2008.08050714

Haney, Craig, Curtis Banks and Philip Zimbardo (2004 [1973])

'A Study of Prisoners and Guards in a Simulated Prison', in Michael Balfour (ed.) Theatre in Prison: Theory and practice, Bristol: Intellect, pp. 19–34.

Hisaki, H. (2015).

Phenomenon of Life and Death by Dōgen and Heidegger––In View of "Embodied Cognition" in Buddhist Philosophy and Phenomenology. *Asian Studies, Vol 3, Iss 1, Pp 105-128 (2015)*, (1), 105. doi:10.4312/as.2015.3.1.105-12

Jung, C. G. (1966).

Psychology and Religion. New Haven:

Yale University Press.

Klein, G. O., Smith, B., & Kitamura, Y. (2010).

Concept Systems and Ontologies: Recommendations for Basic Terminology. *Journal: Japanese Society For Artificial Intelligence* 25(3), 317-325.

Krugman, P. (2014, June 12).

Faith vs. facts when it comes to monetary policy. Retrieved May 9, 2017, from http://www.post-gazette.com/opinion/Op-Ed/ 2014/07/12/ Faith-vs-facts-Gee-monetary-policy-used-to-be-a-pretty-straig stories/201407120030

Lax, P. (1989).

From Cardinals to Chaos: Reflections on the Life and Legacy of Stanislaw Ulam. *Physics Today*, (6), 69.

Lilley, P. (2006). Dirty Dealing :

The Untold Truth About Global Money Laundering, International Crime and Terrorism. London: Kogan Page.

Lipskaya-Velikovsky, L., Jarus, T., Easterbrook, A., & Kotler, M. (2016).

Participation in daily life of people with schizophrenia in comparison to the general population. *Canadian Journal Of Occupational Therapy*, *83*(5), 297-305. doi:10.1177/0008417416647158

McCarley, Robert W. 2016. Studies from Neuroscience

Research Australia Update Current Data on Schizophrenia (Dysregulations of Synaptic Vesicle Trafficking in Schizophrenia). *Mental Health Weekly Digest.*

Messias, E., Chen, C., & Eaton, W. W. (2007, September).

Epidemiology of Schizophrenia: Review of Findings and Myths. Retrieved May 10, 2017, from https://www.ncbi.nlm.nih.gov/pmc/articles/PMC2727721/

Mossman, D., & Steinberg, J. L. (2009). Promoting, Prescribing, and Pushing Pills: Understanding the Lessons of Antipsychotic Drug Litigation. *Journal Of Medicine & Law*, *13*(2), 263-334.

Sanchez, A. H., Lavaysse, L. M., Starr, J. N., & Gard, D. E. (2014).

Daily life evidence of environment-incongruent emotion in schizophrenia. *Psychiatry Research*,*220*89-95. doi:10.1016/j.psychres.2014.07.041

Togar, B., Turkez, H., Tatar, A., Kırkpınar, I.,

Hacımuftuoglu, A., Geyikoglu, F., & ... Dirican, E. (2012).

The genotoxic potentials of some atypical antipsychotic drugs on human lymphocytes. *Toxicology & Industrial Health*, *28*(4), 327. doi: 10.1177/0748233711410919

Uso-Domenech, J. L., & Nescolarde-Selva, J. (2016).

What are Belief Systems?. *Foundations Of Science*, (1), 147. doi:10.1007/s10699-015-9409-z

Vardi, N. (2016, October 07).

Another Drug Company That Raises Prices Like Crazy. Retrieved May 11, 2017, fromhttps://www.forbes.com/sites/nathanvardi/2016/10/06/another-drug-company-that-raises-prices-like-crazy/#7a5386

Wagemans, J., Elder, J. H., Kubovy, M., Palmer, S. E., Peterson, M. A., Singh, M., & von der Heydt, R. (2012).

A century of Gestalt psychology in visual perception: I. Perceptual grouping and figure–ground organization. *Psychological Bulletin*, *138*(6), 1172-1217. doi:10.1037/a0029333

Zimbardo, Philip (2007) The Lucifer Effect: How Good

LIFE AFTER SCHIZOPHRENIA

People Turn Evil, London: Rider.

---

[1]GENE ONTOLOGY (GO) is one of the most operative initiatives in the field in gene ontological research and is a part of the group Gene Ontology Consortium.

About the Author

Anders M. Svenning was born in New York. He started writing with seriousness at the age of nineteen and has now been published in many literary magazines throughout the United States and abroad. Some of the most recent include *Dark Gothic Magazine*, *Adelaide Literary Magazine*, and *Degenerate Literature*. He is the author of *50 States Poetry* (Pansophic Press), *Verdant Grounds, Subtle Boundaries* (Adelaide Books), *Otus in Betulaceæ* (Adelaide Books), *Occipital Circus & Other Stories Regarding Phrenology* (HellBound Books), and *Magisterial Isandore* (Wild Dreams Publishing). Anders M. Svenning lives in Palm City, Florida.